TRUE ADVENTURES

BANDIT'S DAUGHTER

KUNG FU GIRL IN ANCIENT CHINA
HOW MU GUIYING SAVED HER COUNTRY

Simon Mason has written numerous books for younger readers, including *The Quigleys*, *Moon Pie*, and the YA crime thriller series featuring Garvie Smith: *Running Girl*, *Kid Got Shot* and *Hey, Sherlock!*

He has always been fascinated by history, particularly by stories from round the world. He loves to find out how other people have lived.

His interest in China was inspired by his visits to the Ashmolean Museum in Oxford, where he lives, with its stunning collection of Chinese art – some of it 3,000 years old – including delicate writing on animal bone, ceramic figures of camels from the Silk Road and tiny intricate carvings of fantastical animals.

TRUE ADVENTURES

BANDIT'S DAUGHTER

KUNG FU GIRL
IN ANCIENT CHINA

SIMON MASON
With illustrations by Amerigo Pinelli

PUSHKIN CHILDREN'S

Pushkin Press
71–75 Shelton Street
London WC2H 9JQ

The right of Simon Mason to be identified as the author of this Work has been asserted by him in accordance with the Copyright, Designs & Patents Act 1988

Text © 2020 Simon Mason
Illustrations © 2020 Amerigo Pinelli

First published in the UK by Pushkin Press in 2020

1 3 5 7 9 8 6 4 2

ISBN 13: 978-1-78269-273-7

All rights reserved. No part of this publication may be reproduced, stored in a retrieval system or transmitted in any form or by any means, electronic, mechanical, photocopying, recording or otherwise, without prior permission in writing from Pushkin Press

Typeset by Tetragon, London
Printed and bound by CPI Group (UK) Ltd,
Croydon, CR0 4YY

www.pushkinpress.com

BANDIT'S DAUGHTER

Beijing
China
Mount Heng
Liao
Muke Fortress
Furung
Fanshi
Hutuo River
ankou Village
China
Yukou Ditch
Daixian
Town

1

FOREST AMBUSH

The soldiers were hurrying through the deserted forest at dawn when a girl stepped out of the misty trees and stood on the path in front of them. She was wearing a simple village tunic and her feet were bare. She carried nothing in her hands, but stood there lightly, facing them with a calm expression on her face.

The captain raised a gloved fist and the soldiers came to a clattering stop behind him. The birds in the wood were suddenly quiet and there was a second's shocked silence as they all stared wide-eyed at the girl, as if she were a creature from another world. In a moment the soldiers began to mutter among themselves before the captain raised his hand a second time and they were silent again.

The captain was a young man, perhaps no more than twenty years old, clean-shaven, with a wide, lean face and a black ponytail hanging below his helmet. Like the others, he was wearing the uniform of General Yang, with a yellow sash to mark his loyalty to the Emperor of China. His name was Zongbao, which had a good military ring to it when his soldiers addressed him.

Fixing his black eyes on the girl, he opened his mouth, but before he could speak she spoke to him instead.

'What are you doing, hurrying so fast through my forest?'

Her voice was quiet but carried clearly in the silence; the captain was reminded of the rippling sound of running water.

Behind him came a harsh laugh from one of the soldiers.

'It's just a girl!' he heard someone call out.

He turned swiftly and with one look silenced them. They fell into formation again and stood there obediently, awaiting orders.

He tried to recover his composure. 'Listen to me, mountain girl,' he said. 'All this is Imperial land, governed for the Emperor by my father Yang the Peerless of the Daixian fortress. He is guardian of our northern border in the war against the horsemen, and I am here with my men to find the bandit Mu Yu who has stirred up the people and gathered around him so many traitors and malcontents. We are going to find him and discipline him.'

The girl gave him a quiet smile. 'And how will you do that,' she said, 'if even a girl can stop you in your tracks?'

Now he scowled. She was openly making fun of him. 'I have only halted so I can question you,' he said. 'Then we will be on our way. Our mission is urgent. You have heard of this bandit Mu Yu?' he asked her with a severe look. 'This traitor who roams the mountains of Mu Ke, this criminal whose deeds are so vile, this thug, this lowlife, this scum?'

'Yes,' she replied calmly. 'He is my father.'

For a moment he did not know what to say next. At last he spoke. 'If you are telling the truth then you know where we can find him.'

'Of course. Do you think I don't know my own home?'

'Then you will take us there,' he said angrily.

'Well,' she said. 'I might.'

'This is not a request!' he shouted. 'It is a command!'

She nodded thoughtfully, as if considering this. 'All right,' she said at last. 'I will lead you to my father. But only,' she added, 'if you can beat me in unarmed combat.'

There were gasps of disbelief from the soldiers.

'And if I beat *you*,' the girl added, 'I will take you to him *as my prisoner*.'

At that all the soldiers began to shout:

'Give her a spanking!'

'Throw her back in the forest where she came from!'

The captain also heard some laughs. 'He won't dare accept,' he heard someone say with a chuckle. He spun round angrily and once again they fell silent. But when he turned back to face the girl, he found her standing just in front of him. He hadn't heard her move. She must have crossed fifteen paces without making a sound. He saw now how slender she was, how delicate her features. She looked maybe sixteen, seventeen years old, but the top of her head barely came up to his chin. She smiled at him, not as a child smiles but as an adult does, knowingly, and made a sudden movement, a movement so quick her hands were no more than a blur in the air, and his helmet fell onto the path and tumbled away.

She was still smiling, standing motionless again as if she hadn't moved at all. The soldiers behind him were completely quiet now, shocked by her insult.

Captain Yang breathed deeply. 'I accept your terms,' he said to her. 'Prepare to fight!'

UNARMED COMBAT

He felt ridiculous removing his heavy padded jacket, watched by his men. As the son of a famous general, he had been trained in kung fu from an early age. He was powerful and fast and had defeated many champions in competitions. He called over his second-in-command.

'She is only a child,' he said to him in a low voice. 'I will not hurt her. When I have taught her a lesson, treat her fairly.'

'Yes, sir.'

'If she is who she says she is, we will make sure she leads us to the bandit.'

'Yes, sir.'

He hesitated. 'But no one need know about this… contest,' he added in a whisper.

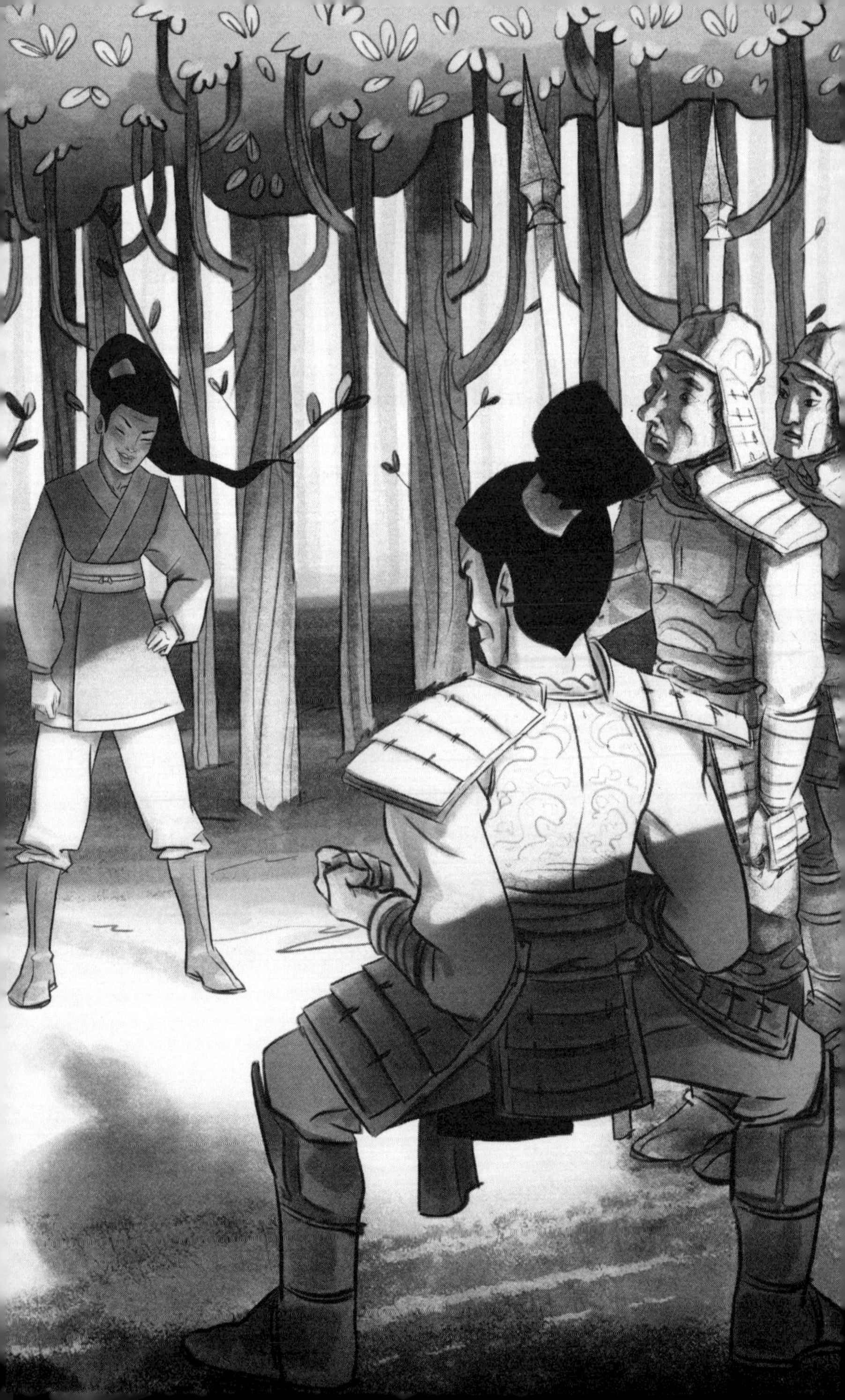

His second-in-command said nothing, and Zongbao turned to face the girl, who still stood on the path, faintly smiling as before.

'If you want to be a proper fighter,' he said, 'you must prepare yourself.'

'I'm always prepared,' she replied.

His men had formed a circle around them and now silence fell again.

The captain crouched in the Horse Stance, legs wide, fists held at his waist. As if mocking him, the girl didn't move at all. Suddenly straightening up, he stepped forward smartly, caught hold of the front of her tunic and lifted her up onto her tiptoes.

'Now learn this,' he said, towering above her. 'The first lesson is to avoid being taken by surprise.' He shook her, though not roughly. 'Enough of this game-playing. You've had your fun. Now you will take us to your father.'

It was odd that even as she dangled from his grip, listening to him, she hadn't stopped smiling. Her right hand suddenly swung up and trapped his fist against her chest. Wrenching back his thumb, in one smooth movement she slammed the back of her fist into his forearm and reversed it swiftly against the side of his head.

Dropping beyond his reach, she stood lightly in front of him again.

For a second he was bewildered. His forearm was numb, his ear buzzing.

A murmur went round the circle of men.

Without any further warnings, he launched into a series of whirlwind kicks, rising, spinning to the left and kicking to the right with the flat of his foot – once, twice, three times – around her head. Changing direction, flattening himself into the Crouch Stance, he spun sideways and rose again, the edge of his right hand slicing towards her neck.

She merely swayed backwards, slapped his hand down with a left chop and brought the same hand up in a fist to punch him twice, with astonishing speed, in the face.

He put his hand up. His nose was bleeding. It dawned on him then that this was no ordinary girl. She stood on the path in front of him, unruffled. An old memory came to him, the rumour of a girl warrior living in the wild. A friend had told him about her one evening. He had paid no attention. He had laughed at it, in fact. Now it came back to him: a girl with unbelievable fighting skills, living in the mountains, almost an animal. And her name came back to him too…

'Mu Guiying,' he said out loud.

She shrugged. His troops began to whisper urgently amongst themselves now.

Now Captain Zongbao began to take the fight seriously. He had been well-trained by his father. Taking up the Empty Stance, he let his mind go still.

He concentrated.

The noises from the soldiers and the birds disappeared; he heard nothing in the silence but the pulse of his *qi*, his vital force, like the sound of water dripping onto stone in an empty mountain cave.

Guiying had adopted the same stance. She was taking it seriously now too. He felt that, whichever way the fight went, it would be over quickly.

He attacked, head down, leaping forward. Before she could react, he stooped and took hold of her behind the knees and flung her backwards. She bounced up almost at once, but he advanced on her, kicking and whirling, as she staggered backwards.

He could hear his men cheering him on.

'Submit!' he cried to her. 'Before it is too late!'

She was stumbling under his heavy blows. For a moment he was almost sorry for her. And then — too late — he realized she wasn't stumbling at all. She was luring him on. As he lunged forward with one last blow she ducked down suddenly under it, hooking her own arm under his groin, catching him off-balance as he flew over her, popping him up into the air with a bump of her tiny shoulders, and sending him on his way, spinning upside down onto the path.

There was proper silence then. Silence in the forest, silence in his head. And when he came to his senses he found himself lying on his back with the girl's foot resting gently but firmly on his throat.

He heard her say to his men, 'One move and I will crush his windpipe.' And then there was quiet again.

And in this quiet he heard himself say, 'I submit.'

3

BANDIT COUNTRY

Mu Guiying was nineteen years old in fact. Old enough to remember her childhood in the Imperial city of Bianjing, capital of the Song Dynasty.

As she walked through the forest with her captive from the Emperor's city, she thought of it: the huge walls patrolled day and night by the Emperor's soldiers, the perfumed gardens where the rich folk crowded to amuse themselves and the busy streets full of shopkeepers and servants. As everybody knew, Bianjing was the biggest city in the world. She also remembered the Emperor's court, the cool shade of the rooms where his officials worked, the splendour of his palace. She had seen the Emperor herself, a fattish, brown-skinned man with baggy eyes and a humorous expression. He was said to be wise, and sometimes bad-tempered. Guiying's father, Mu Yu, used to work for the Emperor and saw him every day.

She would never see the Emperor again. When Guiying was still a child her father had been banished from court in disgrace and sent into exile in the Shandung mountains, where they had lived ever since, among the peasants scraping a living from the woods and lakes.

Captain Yang interrupted her thoughts, calling out to her from the jolting cart where he sat bound and blindfolded.

'Untie me! Untie me now and my father will have mercy on you!'

She merely smiled to herself, and continued along the path, followed by her friends the village people, with the captain complaining in the cart.

They went slowly, hour after hour. Of all China, the north-eastern province of Shanxi was the most beautiful but also the most difficult to navigate. Steep green mountains rose everywhere, thickly covered in forests of evergreen oaks and elm trees. The rocky path wound between them. Sometimes it sank into valleys where a few poor farmers' huts clustered next to dry fields where millet and corn were being grown. Sometimes it rose to the high passes, clinging to the windy mountain sides on natural narrow ledges thousands of metres up, with only the occasional vulture for company.

Few people lived here. On the second day of their journey they passed the last village, Furong. There was a smithy there and sheds for animals and rows of women in the dusty street making bamboo mats. After that, as they slowly went north-east, there was no sign of any habitation at all except for a temple sunk among the greenery and, later, an abandoned quarry of pink limestone. Ahead of them the mountains rose even higher. Towering above them all was Mount Heng, its fearsome peak hidden in mist. Beyond that, to the north, was foreign land belonging to the horsemen, the wandering people of the Great Liao, whose armies had been fighting a terrible war against the Chinese for years.

On the third day Guiying took off the captain's blindfold and he blinked in the sunlight.

'If you try to run away now,' she said, 'you will lose yourself in the mountains and a panther will eat you, which would be a shame. I recommend you stay safe with me.'

The captain said nothing and made no attempt to escape but looked about him alertly as they went. There was a bravery in his eyes that Guiying liked. But she did not think of him. She thought of her father, the bandit Mu Yu, waiting for her in his fortress of Mu Ke.

* * *

They arrived there at the end of the fourth day. The sun was setting over the great Shanyang Ditch, part of the high line of canals built to defend the border against the horsemen of the Liao. The ravine fell away southwards, folded into huge pleats of cliffs and plateaus densely packed with fir trees; and hidden among these trees was her father's fortress built of wood and stone.

Mu Yu was waiting for her at the gates, a short, round, hairy man with flushed cheeks in a rough tunic, not very clean. He had a bad temper and ate too much. When he smiled his teeth were black. From time to time he coughed until he began to shake, and leaned over and spat out a stream of saliva onto the ground.

People stood around him, also rough, also not very clean. Some were old soldiers, some strayed villagers, some simple vagabonds. Women and children and an old Buddhist monk stood among them. There were a few jeers as the cart rumbled to a halt.

Guiying bowed low to greet her father, and he nodded.

'You're late,' he grumbled. 'But you have brought Yang's son.' He wheezed as he spoke.

'Yes, Father. As you commanded.'

He nodded again. Spat on the ground. Then he called over to Captain Yang, 'She fights all right for a girl, doesn't she?'

All his men laughed.

The captain said nothing.

Mu Yu went on, 'Your father, the famous General, wants to be rid of me. He thinks he can exterminate me, like a rat.'

The captain replied, 'My father keeps law and order for the Emperor. All this is the Emperor's land.'

'This is my land,' Mu Yu said. 'I do what I want.'

The captain looked at him defiantly. 'You may have captured me. But I am of no account. My father will send more troops.'

'Your father will do no such thing if he wants to see his son again alive. He will pay me handsomely for your release.'

'My father will never pay you.'

'Then you will die,' the old bandit said.

'I would rather die,' the captain said, 'than have my father give you a penny.'

Mu Yu spat again. 'Put him in the prison,' he said to his men, 'and don't worry about treating him gently. Your father will pay,' he said again to the young man, 'or you will die. Either way, I will be happy.'

And, gesturing for his daughter to accompany him, he turned and waddled back inside his fortress, laughing and joking with his men.

4

THROWN IN JAIL

It took several days to carry a message down from the mountains to the Governor's military town, which lay on a river plain many li to the south. And several more days to wait for an answer. And more days after that to carry a reply back home. All this time Captain Yang lay in the stone hut which served as the bandit's jail.

They had taken away his helmet and his padded jacket, his yellow sash and his boots, and given him a rough linen smock to wear. One of his eyes was bruised from the beating they had given him. As he sat chained to a wooden pole in the centre of the hut, he had plenty of time to think.

After the first few days no one came near him except Guiying, who brought him food. She would set down the wooden bowl of gruel next to him and look at him for a moment, then go away again without speaking, stepping lightly, always with that faint smile on her lips. He became fascinated by her. He had never seen anyone like her before. She made no sound when she moved, and every gesture she made was smooth and calm. Her face was calm too, but her eyes were lively, mischievous even. The way she looked at him made him feel uncomfortable but somehow excited.

Each dawn, through a gap in the hut's wooden door, he watched her carefully wrap her knuckles in an old piece of red cloth, then practise her martial arts in the mud-baked courtyard beyond. He could not believe her grace and strength, tumbling smoothly through her exercises.

He noticed how popular she was in the encampment, how all the people greeted her with respect, even the rough men who served her father.

One day, as she put down his food, she spoke to him. 'Will your father pay to have you freed, do you think?'

'Never,' he replied.

'Then you will die.'

'I welcome it,' he said. 'Better death than disgrace.'

She said no more that day, but the next day she spoke to him again. 'You are a soldier. Have you been fighting in the war?' she asked.

'Yes.'

'Tell me about it. I would like to know.'

He had nothing better to do. To pass the time he described the battles against China's enemy. The horsemen of the Great Liao had been growing in strength for many years. Now they regularly crossed the passes into northern China to burn the villages and kill the people. Zongbao's father, General Yang, was charged by the Emperor to defend China's border. He had succeeded many times in beating back the invaders. But recently there was a new, more dangerous, threat.

'What threat?' Guiying asked.

He hesitated before he answered, and she watched his face intently.

'The army of the Liao have a new battle tactic,' he said at last. 'They call it the Heavenly Gate formation.'

'What is it?'

'A series of seventy-two different moves which their battalions make. Each move is incredibly powerful on its own. Together, they are unbeatable.' He was silent for a while. 'Since they began using the Heavenly Gate we have not beaten them,' he added. 'And now they have given us one hundred days to overcome them in battle, or…'

'Or what?'

'Give up our land.'

Guiying was quiet for a moment. 'Your war sounds difficult,' she said lightly.

His black eyes flashed. '*Our* war,' he said angrily. 'China's war. If the Liao win they will take your father's land too.'

'But it is not his land at all,' she replied. 'You said so yourself.'

When she left him, she was thoughtful however.

More days passed. Still no answer came from General Yang about his son. Guiying's father, the bandit, grew angry. Once he visited the captain in his hut and shouted at him with coarse words and violent gestures until he was red-faced and helpless with coughing. Another time he had the young man dragged into the courtyard, where the women and children made fun of him.

'I will have your pretty head cut off!' Mu Yu yelled.

Still Yang's son would say nothing except that he would rather die than have his father pay for his release. He was defiant, though he looked exhausted. His hair had grown long and matted; on his sharp-boned cheeks was the scrub of a straggly beard.

Every day Guiying and he spoke together a little. Gradually, they got to know each other. The captain asked about her life in the mountains, and she told him of the peaks she had climbed, the rivers she had swum in, the animals she hunted.

'How did you learn to fight?'

'My father taught me at first, when I was a little girl. He was in better shape then, of course. Then a man who came from outside, a friend of my father. I never knew his true name. People here called him Shadow.'

'He must have been skilled.'

'He was a strange man,' she said briefly.

She told him that her father had built the fortress of Mu Ke when she was still a child. He had been unjustly outlawed by the Emperor, and was bitter. He had gathered other discontented men around him. Shadow was one of them. They all hated the Emperor.

The captain asked, 'Before he was a bandit, your father was at the Emperor's court, wasn't he?'

'Yes.'

'I heard he was the Emperor's chief military adviser.'

'Yes, he was.'

'A great tactician, they say.'

She sighed. 'We do not talk of it. My father gets too angry.'

Zongbao nodded but said nothing, and she looked at him thoughtfully.

'Why do *you* talk of it?' she asked.

He said nothing to that either, but there was something in his expression that puzzled her, and once again she went away thoughtful.

THE ONE MAN WHO CAN SAVE CHINA

The next day, after she had brought Captain Yang his bowl of gruel, Guiying sat with him for a while, watching him eat.

When he had finished, she said quietly, 'Why did you come here *really*?'

He paused. 'As I told you, all these mountains are lawless since your father became a bandit. I came here to discipline him.'

She shook her head. 'Tell me the truth.'

They looked at each other in silence; then he sighed. 'All right,' he said. 'There is another reason.' She waited and at last he looked her in the face and explained, 'It is our belief that your father is the one man who can save China.'

She laughed. 'My father is a poor bandit.'

'Have you heard of a man called Lu Zhong?'

She thought for a moment. 'Yes. Once or twice one of my father's men has mentioned him. I remember because my father was so angry to hear his name. Who is he?'

'He was your father's closest friend. Like your father, he was one of the Emperor's chief military advisers. They worked together in Bianjing.'

'What happened to him?'

'He betrayed his country. He went to work for the Great Liao.' Zongbao paused. 'Lu Zhong, may he linger in the tenth court of hell, is the inventor of the Heavenly Gate formation.'

For a long time Guiying was silent. Then she said, 'But what has this got to do with my father?'

'It is said that your father worked for months on a counter-measure, a plan that would beat the Heavenly Gate formation. But then something happened. You say the Emperor sent him here, unfairly, into exile. Others say he fled for reasons of his own, that he is a traitor like his friend. Either way, if he really did work out the counter-measure, he is the one man alive who knows how to defeat the Heavenly Gate. My father sent me here to capture him and take him to the Emperor, to force him to give up his secret.'

He fell silent, and she examined his face for honesty. He was handsome and his eyes were steady but she did not know whether to trust him.

She got to her feet. 'I don't know if I believe you. But I know one thing,' she said sadly.

'What?'

'You have been wasting your time. My father will never help the Emperor. Not any more. Not for your war, not for our war, not for any war. His hatred of him is too deep.'

As she spoke there was the clatter of hooves in the courtyard outside, and a commotion among the people there.

Guiying turned to the captain. 'The messenger has finally returned from your father. There is no more time for talk. Now we will know if you are going to live or die.'

That evening Mu Yu called a council in his great hall. He sat on the raised wooden platform at the end, wheezing and coughing, occasionally sending a stream of saliva into a brass spittoon. Guiying sat behind him. His men lounged at long low wooden tables among the remains of a dinner of noodles, soy beans and yellow wine. Many, like Mu Yu, were dishevelled. Some were drunk.

Mu Yu was a shrewd man for all his coarse expressions and dirty habits. He watched his men for a while, then spoke.

'At last General Yang has sent his reply to us. If his son has been defeated by a girl, he says, he won't pay us a penny. He says we had better go ahead and kill him.'

The men banged their wooden beakers on the tables and Mu Yu raised his hand for them to be silent.

'He thinks we won't dare,' he said.

More banging.

'He thinks we're cowards. He thinks we're animals, living up here in the mountains.'

Thunderous banging.

'Now that I think about it,' he said, 'we *are* animals. So let's kill him, as the old gentleman wishes.'

Prolonged cheers and laughter.

Mu Yu gave the necessary orders.

Later that evening, when Mu Yu had retired to his chamber with a last beaker of rice wine, there was a tap on the paper screen of his doorway and Guiying entered respectfully.

He grunted at her from his mat. 'What is it?'

She sat at his feet. 'Father, is there nothing better we can do with Yang's son?'

He scowled. 'Like what?'

'He knows about the horsemen from the north. He can help us against them if they attack.'

He scoffed. 'The Liao won't attack us.'

'Last year,' she said, 'they burned the village of Furong. If they can burn Furong, they can try to burn Mu Ke.'

'They know we're not friends of the Emperor,' Mu Yu said. 'Their quarrel is not with us,' he said.

'Perhaps their quarrel is with all China,' she said quietly.

'Enough!' her father cried, slapping the floor.

She bowed her head and was silent, and her father continued to drink his wine, glaring at her.

After a while she raised her head again. 'He spoke to me about a battle tactic used by the Liao.'

'What tactic?'

'It is called the Heavenly Gate formation.'

She looked at him and his eyes narrowed as he looked back. He grunted again. 'What of it?'

'He believes you are familiar with it. He came here to get information about it.'

'Then it's worse than I thought!' Her father flung his empty beaker across the room. 'He came here to trick me! To use me!' He was red in the face. 'I should have asked for twice the ransom,' he said. 'No matter. I will feed him to the vultures.'

Guiying began, 'Father—'

'I don't want to hear any more!'

She bowed her head.

Breathing heavily, he wiped his chin. 'The boy Yang dies tomorrow,' he growled. 'Do you understand?'

'Yes, Father.'

She got to her feet, bowed again, and left the room.

6

NOW YOU DIE

The next day was cloudless and still. Soon after sunrise the skies were clear, the forests in the ravine dark in the sharp light. Far overhead, as if news of the execution had travelled across the mountains, a few vultures hung on the mild currents of air.

The courtyard had been swept. In its centre was a shallow round log upturned on its end, and next to it a bucket.

People began to gather. Women brought their children, who sat cross-legged in the dust, waiting solemnly. Mu Yu's men lounged in the sunlight, joking among themselves. Peasants who worked in the woods and the small traders from down the valley and a few of the farmers from further away arrived in small groups and stood nervously in the broad shade of the elm trees surrounding the courtyard. A few chickens ran about. There was a bitter smell of wood smoke from the breakfast fires.

At last Mu Yu appeared smiling, and with him the old monk and the executioner, who carried a sword as tall as himself with a long curved blade and double-handed grip. They took up a position at the wide end of the courtyard and Mu Yu clapped his hands and everyone fell silent.

He wheezed before he spoke. 'When we were driven like beasts into the mountains, we thought we could at least live free,' he said. 'But no. The Emperor has sent his men after us. He wants to hunt us down. He wants to destroy our simple way of life.' He paused as people began to mutter, then he lifted his hands for silence. 'But,' he went on, 'we humbly protest. We don't want to be destroyed. We very humbly send him back a message. *This* is the message.' He clapped his hands again, and a group of men appeared, dragging Captain Yang between them.

He had been beaten again and did not seem to be able to walk properly. His lip was split open. The men hauled him in front of Mu Yu and dropped him on the ground.

Slowly, without taking his eyes off the bandit, the captain struggled painfully to his feet and stood there, chin up.

Mu Yu nodded and spat. 'Yang Zongbao,' he said, 'son of Yang Yanzhou, son of Yang Ye, you are accused of trespassing in our lands and conspiring to murder our people. How do you plead? Doesn't matter,' he added, before Zongbao could speak. 'Guilty as charged. What are we waiting for? Let's get on with it.' He clapped his hands and his men cackled.

The monk stepped forward and Mu Yu waved him back.

'No time for that,' he said. He urged forward the executioner, who went to the upturned log and displayed his sword on the palms of his hands for all to see.

An appreciative murmur went round.

'Do you want to say anything?' Mu Yu asked the captain.

'Yes,' he replied.

'Well, I don't want to hear it,' the bandit said. 'You came here like a thief in the night. You conspired to trick me and to murder me. And you were beaten in a fair fight by a girl. So be silent. Do your work,' he said to the executioner, who took hold of Zongbao roughly.

The captain shook off the man's hand and said loudly to Mu Yu, 'You are a bandit and a traitor, and I am glad my father, loyal servant of the Emperor, will have no dealing with you.'

Mu Yu's face turned a darker shade of red. '*Traitor?*' His rage made him quiver.

'You have betrayed your country,' the captain said. 'I may die now but you will be harshly judged for all eternity.'

The old bandit silenced him. 'Enough!'

All this time Zongbao had not looked once at Guiying, who stood quiet and obedient at her father's side. Now he glanced at her. There was nothing in her face, and he turned from her without another word and allowed himself to be taken to the block, where he was held down by two of Mu Yu's men.

'Now you die,' Mu Yu said. 'I wish to see it happen.'

There was a sudden, profound silence in which the executioner lifted his long sword high into the air. Then Guiying took a quiet step forward into the courtyard, and said, 'Wait.'

Bewildered, the executioner hesitated.

Mu Yu stared at his daughter in confusion.

'You cannot kill him,' she said.

Her father shook his head from side to side. 'Can't kill him?'

'No.'

'Why can't I kill him?'

'Because he is my husband.'

Her father stared at her, twitching slightly.

'We exchanged marriage vows an hour ago,' Guiying said.

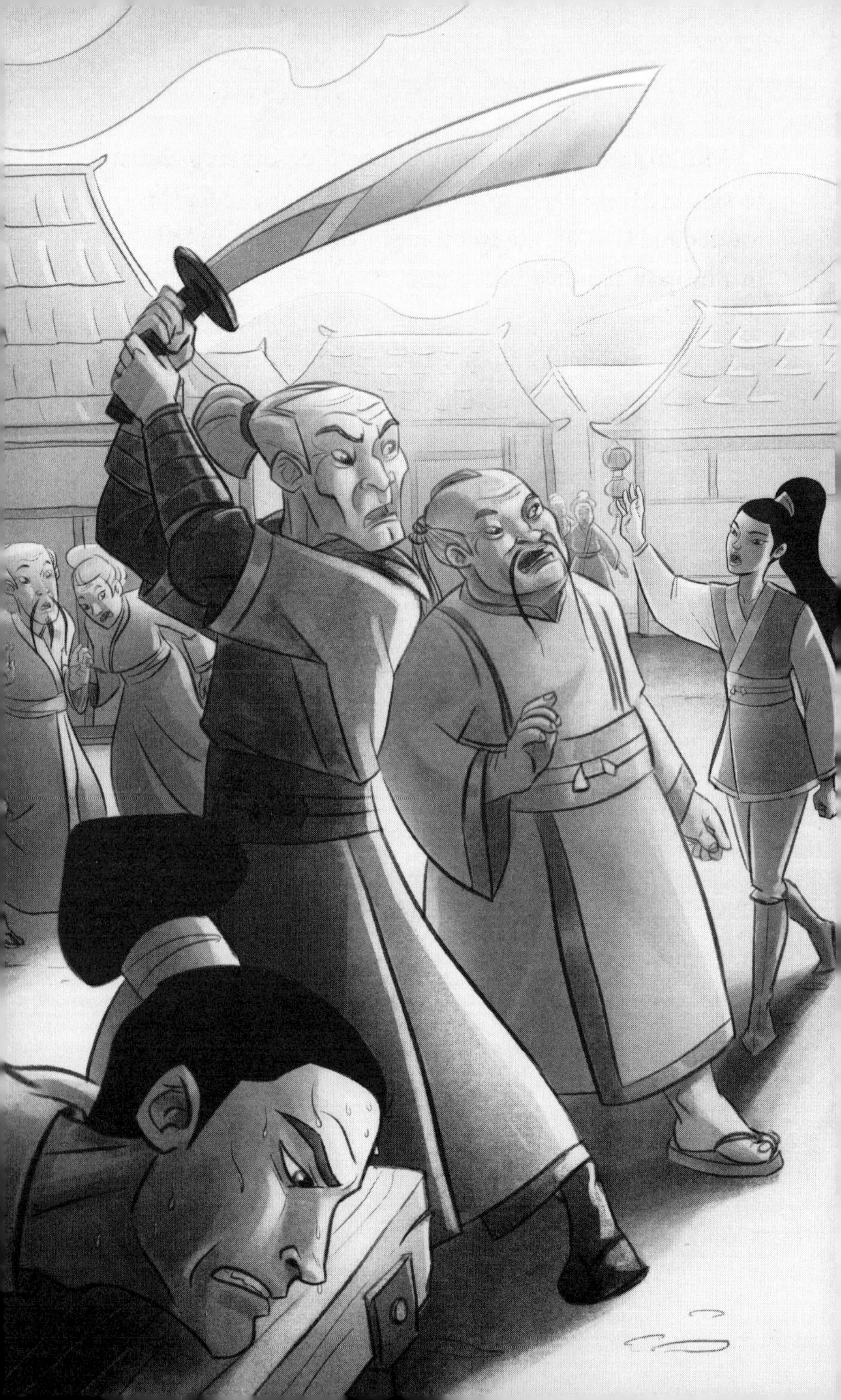

Mu Yu's mouth was open, but he did not seem able to speak. His red face grew redder, his wheezing grew louder and louder. He spluttered, coughed, then fell in a heap in the dust.

7

THE SECRET IS LOST

Mu Guiying nursed her father for nearly a month. All that time he lay immobile in bed, his eyes enormous and wandering, watching her as she went round the room. He had suffered a stroke. Often he tried to speak but he could only grunt like a pig. Whenever she tried to talk to him he shook his head violently and moaned.

Mu Yu's men began to disappear. The few who stayed were content for Guiying and Zongbao to take charge of the fortress. The old bandit had been a harsh ruler.

In the evenings they sat together on the wooden veranda overlooking the ravine of the great ditch. The forests were quiet, the stars clear and bright in the vast sky.

Guiying was calm, as always. But Zongbao was sad.

'Are you unhappy because you married me?' she asked.

He shook his head. 'Of course not. Besides' – he took her hand – 'you saved my life.'

'Are you unhappy because your father refused to pay for your release?'

'No. He would never deal with a traitor, even if his son's life was at stake. He is faithful to his ideals. My father did the right thing.'

'Then why are you unhappy?'

He told her of the battles his father had fought against the Great Liao, desperate clashes high in the mountains, the ambushes, the sieges. Thousands of men had been killed.

Then Zongbao sighed. 'My father is a proud man and very strict. He is the general of all the northern armies, but he trains and eats with the common soldiers. He has an unbreakable code of conduct, and he always does the right thing. And so…'

'So?'

'Unless I take back the knowledge of the countermeasure against the Heavenly Gate, I have failed him. Failed China. And he will act accordingly. We must learn your father's secret.'

'I fear it is too late.'

'We must try.'

* * *

Each day she tried to talk to her father but the sick old bandit only shook his head and made angry noises. Each day he grew a little weaker and at the end of another week, without saying a word, he died.

They took his body out to the burial stone, which stood at the edge of a green plateau overlooking the ravine, and prepared it for the sky burial. The old monk chanted prayers and burned juniper incense; then the people went back to the fortress and left Guiying alone to wait for the birds. Soon they came, slowly gliding in from the north – big griffin vultures with bald heads and long, ruffed necks. They floated down in decreasing circles, and landed with a shuffle and a hop on the burial stone to feast; and when enough of them had gathered to cover her father's remains, Guiying got up and walked back to Mu Ke thoughtfully.

She was sorry her father had died. As was proper in China, she had always obeyed him. Now she was married, the same duty was due to her husband. Duty was important for all girls and women in China. They had to be obedient.

Guiying knew this. But she was different. She solved problems in her own way.

As she walked along the tracks through the fir trees back to the fortress, one thought was fixed in her mind: without the secret of the counter-measure, her husband was in trouble.

* * *

On the veranda that evening, Zongbao said to her, 'We must talk. Your father has died and the secret of the counter-measure has died with him. I have failed in my mission. I must return to my father and report to him. It is my duty.'

She bowed her head.

'And I must go alone,' Zongbao said.

She looked at him with sympathy. 'I understand. We must all be brave in our own way.'

Zongbao nodded. 'There is something else,' he added hesitantly.

'What?'

'I must ask my father's permission for my marriage. This is also my duty. Without his permission, we cannot remain as man and wife.'

He had expected her to be upset, to argue with him, but she was calm, even smiling with that faint smile of hers.

'I know,' she said. 'I have thought of it already.'

She was a constant surprise to him. He said to her passionately, 'I will get his permission. We will be together again, I promise you.'

But she said nothing to that, only smiled a little.

'Go,' she said. 'Go swiftly, and do your duty.'

JOURNEY INTO WAR

The journey took seven days. A guide from Mu Ke went with Zongbao, to lead him down the mountain. They took with them only their weapons and knapsacks filled with cold mutton, yams and tuber onions. Walking all day and sleeping at night in caves used by animals, drinking from the many springs that crossed their path, they followed the Dayu River south, climbed slowly to the high pass across the southern mountain range, and on the morning of the fifth day descended to the broad plain of the Huto River running westward towards the Yellow River. There, Zongbao said farewell to his guide and went on alone, as fast as he could.

He was anxious. He had not seen his father for many weeks. He had heard no news of the war. At the little gold-mining town of Fanshi, three days' march from Daixian Town, he had a shock. Half the buildings were burned to the ground with the smoking trash of homes scattered across the meadows. A peasant told him that the horsemen had pushed deep into Chinese territory, taking the soldiers by surprise. There had been many battles with them and it was only with great difficulty that the Liao had been forced back across the mountains.

'They say they have a new way of fighting,' the peasant said. 'We cannot beat them any more in open battle.'

Zongbao asked about the troops stationed at Daixian.

'Many lost, many wounded.'

'What of the General?'

The peasant shook his head. He didn't know.

Zongbao went on again, faster than ever. Night had fallen on the second day by the time the garrison town came into view ahead, watchfires blazing on its walls and in the towers of the fortress above it, and it was almost midnight before he found himself approaching the familiar gates.

He did not reach them. Half a dozen guards came swiftly out of the shadows and surrounded him and he was told in a harsh voice to surrender his weapons.

When he gave the marshal his name, the man simply scowled. 'We have been expecting you,' he said. 'We have instructions to escort you under armed guard to the citadel.'

'Are these my father's orders?' Zongbao asked, surprised.

The stern-faced marshal made no reply.

'What has happened?' Zongbao said in sudden fear.

But he was seized by the guards and frogmarched away.

There was a sort of fretful quiet in the streets. Groups of people stood together in the shadows, whispering. In places, soldiers were sleeping with their weapons, or lying wounded on coarse linen stretchers. In the main square a barricade had been built of old carts and sacks of earth. Everywhere was an air of fearfulness.

Zongbao expected to go to his father's residence, the Governor's House, but he was taken instead up the hill to the fortress, where he was put into one of the public rooms, watched suspiciously by two of his father's personal bodyguards while he waited.

The hours passed slowly. Zongbao squatted on the floor, trying to remain calm. Everywhere in the town he had seen the signs of exhaustion and defeat. He did not know if his father was alive or dead. He thought of Guiying, so many miles away, and felt lonelier than ever.

It was the early hours of the morning before the great double doors at the end of the room crashed open, and Zongbao stood to attention.

His father appeared.

'Father!' Zongbao cried with relief. But his father made no reply.

General Yang was not yet forty years old, a lean, muscular man in his prime, with a stern face and close-cropped black hair. All his movements were unhesitating and efficient. Walking into the room, it took him only a few seconds to dismiss the guards, acknowledge his son, and take up a position in front of the great table, legs apart, arms folded across his chest, already awaiting his son's report.

Zongbao bowed deeply and respectfully. 'Father,' he said, and lifted his head. 'Before I speak, tell me, please, what has been happening here? There are extra guards posted at the gates, and barricades built inside the city. Are you expecting an attack?'

The General's hard and watchful face betrayed no emotion but Zongbao could see how tired he was. After a moment of thought, his father spoke briefly.

'Seventeen days ago, the horsemen of the Liao made a great assault. They came down through the Yanmen Pass, killing all in their path, moving eastward through the villages, as far as Fanshi. Now they have retreated again, into the mountains, but we believe they have left behind spies and assassins ready to strike us at any moment. This is why we are vigilant.'

'What happened at Fanshi? I saw the burned buildings. Did you beat them?'

'We stopped them. We did not beat them.' The General cleared his throat. 'For forty-eight hours without rest we fought them but could not defeat them, and in the end they set fire to the town while we could only watch. It was their message to us, they said.'

'What message?'

'That the one hundred days have nearly passed. The next time they come, they will burn all the towns from here to the Yellow River. And that is why,' he said, fixing his son with a stern gaze, 'we need the counter-measure. So reassure me,' he said. 'Tell me that you have brought with you the secret of it. Quickly, now.'

Zongbao went pale. 'Father,' he said at last. 'The secret is lost. I have failed. I am sorry.'

There was a long moment of silence in the room.

'I cannot hear this,' the General said.

'It is true.'

The General said, 'The Yangs have guarded this border for the Emperor for three generations. We have pledged to keep our country safe from the horsemen. Your grandfather, Yang Ye, hero of the Battle of Yanmen Pass, gave his life at Chenjiagu.'

Zongbao flinched at the sound of the name. It was famous as one of the bitterest defeats against the Great Liao.

'I know, Father.'

'Our duty is clear. Failure is unacceptable.'

'Yes, Father.'

'You are my son. You know this.' He hesitated, just a moment. 'I love you. But I must treat you like any other soldier.'

'I know.'

'You allowed yourself to be captured. Your mission has been a failure. Before I summon the guards, is there anything else you wish to tell me?'

'Yes, Father.'

'What is it?'

Zongbao swallowed nervously. 'I… I am married.' There was another long silence after he said that. 'I mean,' he added, 'I wish to ask for your permission.'

The General said nothing. A muscle jumped in his cheek. His eyes blazed.

'Father,' Zongbao said in a rush, 'I know she would not be the match you wanted for me. She is the bandit's daughter, I admit. But you cannot judge her. She is like no one else. She—'

The General held up his hand, and his son was silent. '*The bandit's daughter?*' the General said slowly, as if he could not believe it.

Zongbao bowed his head.

'Then I do judge her,' the General said. 'I must. And I must judge you too.' He clapped his hands, and his guards came in. 'Take Captain Yang to the cells,' he said curtly, and turned away.

9

A SURPRISE FOR THE GENERAL

As he walked through the streets to his private quarters in the Governor's House, accompanied by his personal bodyguard, General Yang's heart was heavy. He was perplexed and disheartened by his son's behaviour but he could not allow personal sorrow to occupy his thoughts. He walked briskly on. The night was clouded and dark. The breeze carried the stink of ash all the way from Fanshi up the valley, and his expression hardened as he thought of the villagers who had died there.

Guards stationed at street corners saluted him as he passed.

At the entrance to his house he paused to question one of them. 'All quiet?'

'Yes, sir.'

'Nothing to report?'

'False alarm at the north gate an hour ago. Nothing else.'

The General hesitated. 'What false alarm?'

'Street boy breaking the curfew. Wouldn't stop when challenged. Just a child. His voice hadn't even broken. No danger, sir.'

The General nodded. His thoughts were elsewhere. 'How many men on guard tonight?'

'A dozen, sir. The best.'

He nodded. Leaving them all outside, he went alone into the house. It was only four hours from dawn now and he was very tired. But there was still work to be done, so he went into his study and he began to write a letter at his desk.

It was a letter to his marshals, telling them that when the Great Liao attacked again it was their duty to fight without surrender to the death. He concentrated hard to find the right words. Half an hour passed. Once there was a noise in the corridor outside but he merely paused, then carried on writing.

At last he finished the letter. He sealed it and, finally looking up, was astonished to see a strange girl relaxing on the other side of the desk, no more than an arm's length from him. She seemed to have been there for some time.

For a moment he doubted his sanity and could not speak.

She spoke to him instead. 'General Yang,' she said politely. 'I have been waiting to talk to you. I didn't want to interrupt you while you were working.'

His brain began to work again. Could the Great Liao have started to use female assassins? He glanced swiftly towards the door.

The girl smiled at him. 'The guard outside is no longer conscious,' she said. 'Nor the guards on the stairs or at the front door. Do not worry. They will recover.'

He listened to her with amazement. 'Who are you?' he asked.

'Your daughter-in-law.'

At last he found his voice. 'The bandit's daughter?'

She nodded. 'By now,' she said, 'my husband will have asked your permission for his marriage and you will have refused it and he will be in your prison.'

He looked at her sternly. 'That is correct.'

'I wish you to give your son your permission.'

'You have come here to ask me this?'

'Yes.'

'It is not usual.'

'I am not usual.'

'I can see that.'

He stood, and she stood too, to face him.

'Your father is a traitor,' the General said severely.

'My father is dead. The burial birds have taken him.'

The General narrowed his eyes. 'Now I understand what my son told me. The secret of the counter-measure died with him. First, your father betrayed his country; now he has kept from us the only weapon with which we could have defended ourselves.'
He added bitterly, 'His duty, like mine, was to his Emperor.'

'I know you are a man of honour.'

'Unlike your father. He failed in his duty. He did not even understand duty. Nor,' he said sternly, 'does his daughter.'

'I understand my duty very well. It is to my husband now.'

'He is not your husband, for I have not given permission!'

'Then give it, to allow me to do my duty.'

There were hurried footsteps in the corridor outside and a guard called out anxiously, 'General! Are you all right? I heard shouting.'

Guiying said softly, 'You can call your men in to help if you need them to protect you from an unarmed girl. Go ahead. A dozen strong men should do it, if they work together.'

The General frowned.

She went on, 'We have a difficulty. Let me suggest a solution. You are a man of honour, so you will accept a private challenge, fighter to fighter. Here and now. If you win I will walk into your prison myself.

If *I* win, you set your son free and give him your blessing. There is no need of a referee. I trust you. And, after all, I'm only a girl. But I should warn you. I made a similar offer to your son and he lost.' She bowed respectfully.

For a moment the General stood staring at her in fury. Then he barked at the door, 'Guard! There is no need to distress yourself. All is in order. You may retire.'

Together, the General and Guiying listened to the soldier's footsteps fading down the hallway, and when there was complete silence, Guiying said, 'Shall we begin?'

10

NO MERCY

They took up their positions facing each other, and bowed. On one side of them was the desk, on the other the wooden wall with the fireplace and two bookcases. Hanging on the wall above the fire was a short curved sword in a worn leather scabbard. Behind Guiying was a couch and footstool. Behind the General was a small wooden table and a brass stand with a clock on it. Other items – a cupboard with a pile of maps on it, a saddle, a split-bamboo broom – were placed haphazardly around the room.

This was the arena in which they would fight.

Watching her all the time, the General carefully wrapped grey bandages round the knuckles of both hands and took up the Horse Stance, fists held tightly in front of him. Guiying, as usual, adopted the looser

Sparring Stance, knees slightly bent, palms held outwards.

The General did not move. He locked his eyes on hers. Several minutes passed, each of them unmoving, then at last, as if suddenly wafted into the air, Guiying floated forward with a series of flickering punches. He blocked her blows with his forearms and elbows. Without pause, she spun on tiptoe into a roundhouse kick, which he parried with his left fist. Dropping for an instant into a crouch, she rose suddenly in front of him, punching rapidly from the shoulders into his face, and he blocked all her blows with his palms, calmly and efficiently.

He stood unmoving again, in the Horse Stance, his eyes still locked on hers.

Neither of them had made a sound so far, except for the slap and crack of their hands and feet. She could see that the General was a fighter of the old school, disciplined, tight in his movements and ever-watchful. His defence was absolutely firm. But he made no move to attack her. He merely waited sternly, in the Horse Stance position.

She remained light and loose. Circling him smoothly, she forced him to shift round, step by step, until he stood with his back to the fire, unable to retreat. Then she took him by surprise with a hook kick and the sole of her tiny right foot slapped him with a smart crack across his face.

His cheek flushed red. After a moment he spoke. 'I understand,' he said. 'This is your message to me. We both know that you could have knocked me out with your heel.'

'Next time I will,' she said. 'You do not attack me because I am a girl. You hope I will dance around and trip myself up. So I tell you this. I do not trip. I want no mercy. Do not fight me as a girl. Fight me as an equal. If you don't, next time I catch you, you won't get up.'

The General gave a slight nod. 'So be it. No mercy.'

She saw in his eyes that he meant it. And a moment later he came at her hard. He was fast as well as powerful. His first punch took her by surprise, catching her in the middle of her chest, and she gasped. As she reeled backwards, he kicked outwards against her knee and she staggered sideways. She punched from the hip to his stomach, but he blocked it with a downward chop to her forearm, then stepped across her at an angle, chopping to her throat and elbow-punching the underside of her nose.

As she spun out of his grip, she raked his side and face with stinging crane flicks of her stiffened fingers, her own speed driving him backwards towards the fire again.

They faced each other, panting.

Without any change in his expression, the General reached behind him and took down the sword from the wall, and in one wide arc sliced it turning and twisting towards her.

'As you requested,' he said in an even voice, 'no mercy.'

She retreated as he advanced, swaying to escape his thrusts. She could see in his eyes nothing but the steely determination to defeat her, kill her if necessary.

The brass stand with the clock on it overturned with a crash. The cupboard splintered in two and the rolled-up maps spun into the air. As she fell, the General was on her at once, slicing down at her. In a moment she had grabbed the broom that was propped against the wall, and with it parried the savage blows of his sword, fighting her way slowly to her feet.

Round the wreckage of the furniture, they circled each other, trading blows, sword against broom. Shreds of bamboo flew into their faces.

In the hall outside there were shouts and running feet, but Guiying and the General ignored them, fighting on with utter concentration. Both were tired.

The General went for the kill. Flourishing his sword, he twirled towards her. She jumped over one sweep, ducked under another, and, as he came close to deliver a headbutt, snap kicked his standing foot. The broom cracked across his knuckles, and his sword went clattering across the wooden floor. He lunged towards her with a roundhouse punch, but found the

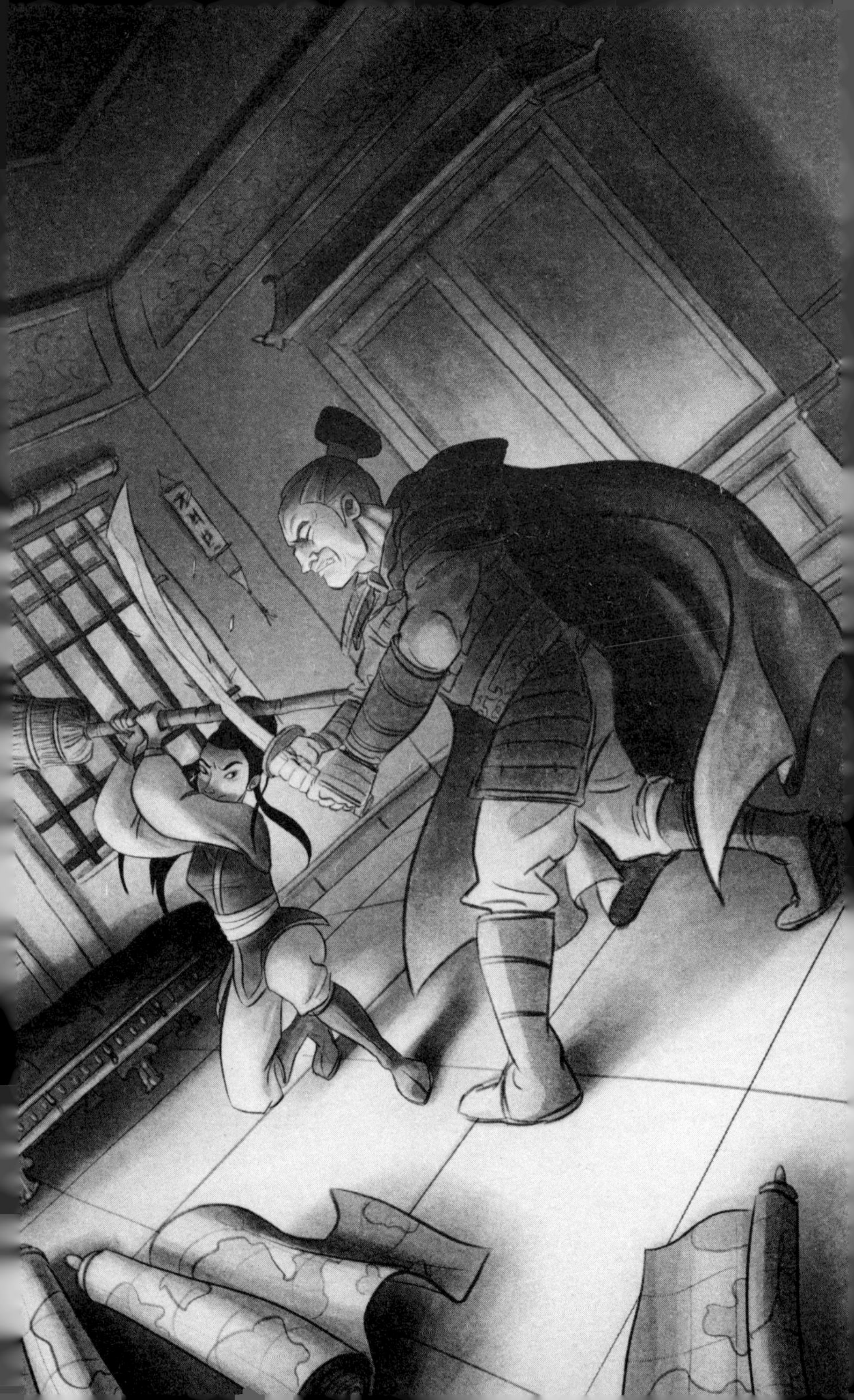

splintered end of the broom handle at his throat, and he froze, arms outstretched.

At that moment his soldiers burst through the door.

Guiying at once dropped to the floor, laying herself at the General's feet. 'Grant my request, General,' she said in her most respectful voice, 'and I offer myself to serve you all my life, to the confusion of your enemies.'

And the soldiers stood there, mouths open, looking in bewilderment at the scene in front of them.

11

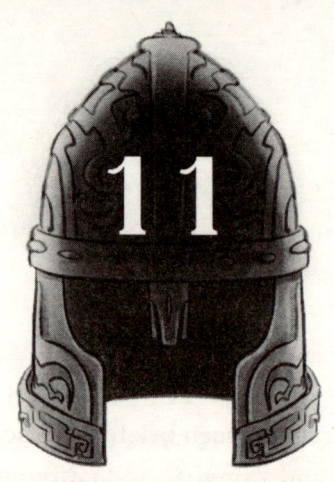

ENEMY ON THE MOVE

'**G**eneral, sir,' one of them said at last. 'We bring news.'

Instantly the General gave him his attention. 'What is it?'

'The Great Liao are on the move again. We captured their scouts in the valley this side of the Guanguo river. Their army is big.' He hesitated.

'How big?' the General asked.

'More than fifty thousand men.'

The General nodded. 'Fetch my son from the prison. We have work to do.'

The guards hesitated.

'What is it?'

They looked towards Guiying. 'Sir. The girl…?'

'The girl stays here.' He was already striding back to his desk.

Dawn was breaking, a grey smear of light outlining the window screens, birdsong scratching the silence as they sat facing each other in the General's darkened study.

The General had been briefed by the scouts. He began to talk and Zongbao and Guiying listened to him.

In the last few months, the General said, the Great Liao had become bolder, almost insulting, raiding Chinese territory at will. They had come from the east along the river valleys as far as Fanshi, and southwards over the mountains, burning towns as they went. Now they had silently slipped through the Yanmen Pass and were camped outside Wujiayao.

'Only two days' ride away!' Zongbao exclaimed.

His father nodded gravely. 'And the peasant villages in the valley below them are undefended. We must prepare to go to their aid.'

It would not be easy, he explained. The odds were heavily against them, and after their recent defeats his men were tired and fearful.

'The Liao are fierce and ruthless. Their general, Xiao Dalin, is a brilliant tactician. They move fast – and they know they can beat us.'

Guiying asked, 'Because of their new formation?'

He nodded. 'Their cavalry is strong, crossbowmen deadly, their winged-tiger infantry unmatched in hand-to-hand fighting. But what makes them so powerful is their organization. This is the secret of their success. Their vanguards and wings combine with such speed into bewildering new formations. We cannot resist them.' He gestured to his desk. 'Last night I was writing to tell my commanders that the time we face the Liao in a final reckoning is coming very soon. I fear that now it is here. The great moment of our lives. At stake, China's very existence.'

It was quiet in the little room. Outside, they could hear noises of men rising wearily to a new day of fear.

The General looked at Guiying. 'I am sorry. You have chosen a difficult time to join us,' he said. 'Our family's job is to guard the northern border.'

She nodded respectfully. 'I have heard this,' she said. 'Though I have never known why.'

The General looked at her. 'The Emperor himself entrusted my father, Yang Ye, with the task. Listen, and I will tell you how it happened.'

DEFENDERS OF THE NORTHERN BORDER

He began.
'When he was a boy, my father was a hunter with dogs and falcons in these forests. When he became a man, he was a fighter for the Lord of the Northern Han — mountain people trying to protect themselves against two mighty forces, the horsemen of the Great Liao to the north and the Song dynasty to the south. Bloody times — the Era of the Five Dynasties and Ten Kingdoms, warlord fighting against warlord.

'A generation ago, in the third year of the old Emperor, in the long, hot summer month of the goat, the Song army besieged the Han capital of the Dragon City Jinyang. My father's lord, Shizu, surrendered.

'My father did not. He had received no instruction. Hour after hour he fought alone against the Emperor's army. Only when Shizu ordered him to lay down his arms did he obey. He wept then at his defeat, bowed to the north, took off his armour, laid it on the ground and knelt before the Emperor.

'He expected to be killed, of course. But the Emperor knew a brave man when he saw one, and he made my father Imperial Defender of the Northern Border. From that moment my father's enemy was the Great Liao. Many times he fought them. At Yanmen he won a famous victory.'

'All China has heard of it,' Guiying said.

The General nodded. 'Wild Goose Pass is where it happened, a narrow passage fortified by three gatehouses high in the mountains between the valleys of Shanxi and the northern steppes. There is no other way through the snowy peaks. But my father knew it well from his hunting days. Taking his best and bravest soldiers, he led them up the rock face to the north of the pass and arrived above the horsemen's army. There they hid until my father's comrade General Pan Mei launched a frontal assault; then my father and his men fell on the Great Liao from behind. The destruction was complete. The Liao Emperor's brother-in-law was killed, his general captured.'

The General nodded again, with satisfaction.

'Ever afterwards, the Liao called my father "Yang the Invincible". He was a tough man but fair. When his soldiers had no food he went without food too. When there was no firewood for them he lit no fire himself, camping in the mountains with them high above the snowline. Discipline was everything to him. Whenever the Liao saw his flag they retreated at once. But,' he went on, 'this did not last for long. The Liao were only waiting for the opportunity to take their revenge. Fifteen years ago my father was caught by superior forces north of here.

'It happened like this. Cao Bin, a good but unlucky general, had been defeated by a huge Liao army, which moved swiftly westward to threaten the whole province. Outnumbered, my father requested permission to evacuate civilians in a strategic retreat. But the Emperor's military adviser Wang Shen refused. He was ordered to attack at once with the few men he had.'

'Did the order come from the Emperor?' Guiying asked.

The General hesitated. 'My father had no choice but to assume it did,' he said at last. 'In any case, it was, shall we say, an unfortunate order. He was forced into a suicidal engagement with the much larger Liao army at Chenjiagu. Reinforcements had been promised by Pan Mei, but they never arrived. He was cut off, his position hopeless. He was captured. Refusing to co-operate, within three days he starved himself to death, and his head was presented to the Liao Emperor and his mother the Empress Dowager, who hates the Chinese above all things. So the Liao had their revenge at last.'

There was silence after he said this.

Guiying bowed her head. 'The account of such a defeat must have been a terrible thing for his son to hear,' she said with sympathy.

'I did not hear it. I *saw* it. The day of the battle I had the honour to be vanguard commander.' He rolled up the sleeve of his tunic and showed his forearm gristly with scar tissue. 'I was wounded by an arrow and taken from the field,' he said bitterly. 'Five of my brothers died that day. Three survived. One betrayed China by going over to the Great Liao. One became a monk and lives in a monastery far away where war cannot disturb him. I am the last. With my father dead, the new Emperor entrusted me with his work. Now I am Defender of the Northern Border in my turn. As my son will be in his.'

He fell quiet. From outside came crackling sounds of cooking, the sweet, harsh smell of smoke from the camphor wood fires and low muttered voices.

Zongbao said proudly to Guiying, 'My father has won his own victories. The Liao have a name for him too: *Yang the Peerless*.'

General Yang acknowledged it. 'It is a hard task,' he said. 'But I am glad to fulfil my duty to my Emperor.'

Guiying said, 'I have a question. You may not like it.'

'Ask me anyway. I'm getting used to your rudeness.'

'You are the Emperor's loyal soldier, but does the Emperor have faith in you?'

General Yang looked at her fiercely, but for a long time made no reply. Finally, turning his face away, he said in a low voice, 'I do not know. I do not often hear from court.'

'Have you received reinforcements, supplies, weapons to replace those you have lost?'

He shook his head. 'My messages go through the Emperor's new military adviser Fu Xian. He commands forces to the south, where there is no fighting. He tells me there are no troops to spare, that the Emperor is displeased I should request them. But the truth is, over the years we have been weakened. Since the defeat at Chenjiagu there are many senior positions in the army we cannot fill. They have been taken, temporarily, by the widows of my dead brothers. They call them the "Women Generals". Fearless, honourable people. You will see Ye's widow, my mother. She carries with her everywhere a dragon-headed cane. But of course,' he said, 'these ladies cannot fight. They are not men.'

Guiying said nothing to that.

'Father,' Zongbao said. 'Allow me now to continue our story.'

The General nodded and his son began to speak.

13

THE ENEMY GROWS STRONG

'For many years,' Zongbao began, 'my father has worked tirelessly to rebuild towns, to replant the fields, restore the watermills and repair the smithies. He has shored up the river bulwarks against the yearly flooding. He has made many improvements to the lives of the villagers. But, as you know now, the Liao have attacked us more and more frequently. My father has done his best to resist them.

'A few years ago he was besieged inside the small town of Suicheng without any soldiers at all. Not one. The Liao soldiers jeered at him, waiting for him to surrender. But nothing was further from his mind. Every morning before sunrise he silently trained the townsfolk in the basic skills of combat. Every evening after dark they made their own weapons from the melted-down iron of old cart axles, armour out of leather saddles and catapults from the guts of cats. Most importantly of all, he gave them belief. And when they were ready these townsfolk took the Liao soldiers by surprise and drove them away.'

Guiying smiled. 'I would like to have seen that. Surely then,' she said, 'the Emperor was pleased with your father.'

Zongbao's face darkened. 'Fu Xian only scolded him for keeping the peasants from their work in the fields.' He frowned. 'Another time,' he went on, 'my father and a dozen hand-picked men lured the Liao army westward through the mountains to a place called Yangshan, a rocky crater hidden in the folds of the ravines, easy to get into, almost impossible to get out of. There his army destroyed the enemy forces in an ambush, and to the Emperor he sent the head of the Liao general himself.'

Guiying was watching the General's face, which did not change its brooding expression. 'And what did the Emperor say to that?' she asked quietly.

General Yang merely shook his head. The Emperor had sent no word, his son explained. The only response from Fu had been an instruction to fall back into position without delay.

'And now,' Zongbao said, 'the Liao have the Heavenly Gate formation. Every week they become bolder. We lose men and become weaker. We must find a way to resist them, or China will fall.'

The General got to his feet. 'So, enough of these tales of the past. My son is correct. We must think now of the present, however painful that is. We have no counter-measure. But there is work to be done, there are villages to defend.'

He looked from Zongbao to Guiying standing before him.

'I tell you this,' he said, his eyes beginning to blaze. 'It is our duty – and an honour – to defend the northern border. The Emperor expects the job to be done. So do I.' He paused and looked hard into Guiying's eyes. 'But we need also to face the truth. The enemy is mighty and we fight against them alone. Our last real hope was to find the counter-measure. We have failed. But let us make our final stand and, if victory is impossible, find the courage for desperate resistance and honourable death in the service of the Emperor and our people.'

Zongbao snapped to attention and saluted his father.

Guiying sighed. 'I don't think we should be too gloomy,' she said.

The General glared at her. 'And why not?'

'Well,' she said, 'the thing is, *I* know the counter-measure.'

14

A SECRET REVEALED

They stared at her in silence.

Zongbao's mouth fell open. 'But...'

'What?'

'*Why didn't you say?*'

'You never asked me,' she said simply. 'Strange. It's as if you think that women know nothing about fighting.'

They continued to stare.

Guiying went on. 'There are two issues, however.'

'What issues?'

'The counter-measure is incomplete. The very last part is missing. My father hadn't worked it out by the time he was exiled. Once he was in the mountains he was too angry and bitter to think about it any more.'

The General said, 'Then we will have to work it out ourselves from what you know. What's the second issue?'

'I would like to be involved in the fighting.'

Now the General frowned.

Zongbao looked at his father. 'Sir, I know it is not usual, but—'

The General held his hand up to silence him. 'Yes, I know. *She* is not usual. I have discovered this already.'

Guiying said, 'It will not be so unusual. You already have women generals. Fearless, honourable people, you said. No, I am not a man. I am Mu Guiying, bandit's daughter. And I fight.'

The General frowned. 'I know that too. But it has not been done before. What will the men say? How will they react?'

She shrugged.

The General stood there in silence, thinking.

She said, 'Would it help if I put things in a slightly different way?'

'Please.'

'I won't tell you the secret of the counter-measure if you don't let me fight.'

The General and his son looked at each other.

'Preferably,' she added, 'in command.'

The General clenched and unclenched his fists. He gave a deep sigh and nodded; and the next moment he was striding back to his desk.

'Summon the battalion commanders,' he said to his son. 'Bring me the maps of the river valleys to the north. We have no time to lose.'

15

HOW TO DO A SNAP KICK

Within an hour preparations had begun. In the wide dirt courtyard in the centre of town they gathered, battalion after battalion, weary soldiers who had been defeated many times by the Liao. Fear showed in their faces as they stood in quiet rows between the Governor's Residence and the low thatched workshops of the smiths and tanners, listening to the General deliver his instructions, his clear voice carrying on the breeze. What they needed was hope. He gave it to them without disguising the truth.

The Great Liao had moved suddenly into position up at Yanmen Pass, he told them, a great horde. Their purpose was clear: to sweep down to the plain below with maximum destruction. Directly in their path lay the pretty village of Nankou, famous for its children's parties in the summer in honour of Shennong, the peasant god who first taught men to farm.

'The children of Nankou need us now,' the General said. 'Are we going to fail them?'

He looked around the courtyard as the men murmured half-heartedly.

'I will not lie to you,' he said quietly. 'The Liao outnumber us. Their armour and weapons are superior to ours. Yes,' he said, slowly nodding. 'I see things as you do. What am I to say? Our task is impossible? Perhaps it is.' He examined their faces. 'But,' he went on, 'I also say this. Because it's *you*, I think you can do it anyway. Yes,' he said, looking keenly at them all. 'And the children of Nankou think so too. Because you are the men who can do the impossible. And I am proud to stand with you because, together, *we will not fail.*'

And as they went away with their commanders into the packed dirt fields under the city walls to begin their preparation, the soldiers felt a sombre determination to succeed or die in the attempt.

One thing puzzled them: the strange girl who had been standing next to Captain Yang at the General's side. Not tall, quite slender. Standing there with a quiet, casual confidence, returning the men's glances with unusual boldness. No one knew who she was. Not even the General's granddaughter would have been allowed to attend a military briefing. It was a mystery. The men didn't like it – her presence made them uneasy. They glanced towards her darkly. Everyone knew that women were unlucky in a battle campaign.

All day, while preparations were made for the journey, the infantry trained. The commanders worked them hard. In the fight ahead there would be plenty of hand-to-hand combat. They practised their throws and blocks, their punches, chops and jabs. For over an hour they practised kicks, watched by their commanders and, from where she stood quietly in the shadow of a vegetable-seller's stall, by Guiying.

She was watching three men in particular. Their names were Ying, Ju and Lun. Ying was the shortest, a wiry man with an egg-shaped head and lank hair drooping to his shoulders. He was nimble in his movements but careless. Ju was sturdier, wide-hipped and flat-faced; he kicked out doggedly with slow, steady blows. Lun was a giant with too much belly, stooped and long-armed, but surprisingly quick on his feet and watchful with small glinting eyes. His kicks were lumbering but huge.

He was bad-tempered. As he sparred, glancing towards Guiying, he muttered loudly about women who didn't know their place. In time the men around him began to mutter too.

'They should stay in the kitchen,' Lun grunted. 'That's all they're good for.' He spat and wiped his chin, then, noticing Ju drop his guard, booted him suddenly in the midriff. 'You're as bad as a woman yourself,' he said as Ju rolled choking in the dirt. 'There's no one in this tinpot army who can give me a fight.'

Turning with a sullen laugh, he almost stumbled over Guiying, who had silently taken up a position behind him. Her knuckles were wrapped in a red cloth.

In surprise he stared at her dumbly. Other men nearby stopped their training and stared at her too.

'I've got a message for you from the kitchen,' she said softly.

Lun frowned.

'*This* is the message.' Suddenly bouncing up and lifting a knee, she flicked out a foot and lashed him under the nose, then stood again at ease.

For a moment he didn't seem to realize what had happened.

'Your nose,' she said helpfully.

Grunting with pain, Lun clutched his face with a big hand and drew it away to see it covered in blood, which he stared at with amazement.

'That was the snap kick,' she said. 'Now for message number two. The roundhouse kick.'

Pivoting on her left foot, she spun round, leaping lightly into the air and whipped her right foot high and wide through 180 degrees to the point where it met the side of Lun's head with a noise like a snapping branch.

This time he didn't need to be told what to do. He staggered sideways with a roar.

'Good,' she said. 'You're getting the hang of it. Message number three. Hook kick.'

He didn't wait for it. He charged her, head down, arms swinging, and she disappeared. Confused, he looked about him wildly, and she appeared again, suspended in mid-air slightly to one side of him and thrashed her left foot against his right temple.

When his eyes cleared and he could see again, she was lolling just within reach, but the pain made him wary and he stayed back. Glancing round at the other men he saw the same confusion in their eyes.

'Better and better,' she said to him. 'Your turn now. Butterfly kick. Come, take my head off.'

He wiped the blood out of his eyes and considered the situation. A cunning look came into his face. Waiting until he saw her relax, he lurched forward suddenly, stamping his foot heavily into the air where she had just been, and crashed forward with a bellow into the dirt.

'Side heel kick,' she said, bending over him. 'Good use of surprise. I like your style. My turn again.'

He was back on his feet, swaying and panting.

'Outside lotus kick,' she said, adopting the Bow Stance.

Despite his pain, he found his voice. 'Never heard of it,' he muttered.

'Like this,' she replied with a smile, turning her back on him, stepping away, then spinning round suddenly towards him again, almost upside down, and scything her left foot upwards into his jaw.

Slowly he got up a second time. He didn't want to but he wasn't a quitter. The girl, however, made no further move.

'I like you,' she said to him. 'You're big and strong and you don't give up, even when faced by superior opposition. You will be a hero in the fight tomorrow. What the Liao have done you will avenge.'

He stared at her, dazed. 'Who are you?' he asked brokenly.

'Your commanding officer,' she replied. 'I thank you for your time. You may continue with your training.'

And she walked away, back to the vegetable-seller's stall.

The day ended with great tiredness. Night fell over the town. Everyone knew that the next day they would march north to the greatest fight of their lives.

There was no rest for the General and the captain, his son, however. Long after nightfall they talked together in the General's study, reviewing their battle plans by candlelight, speaking softly in the quiet room.

Standing upright in front of the shuttered window, the General expressed his worry. 'The formations of the counter-measure are complicated,' he said. 'Nor are they complete. Worse, they are completely untested. How do we know they will help us?'

Zongbao replied, 'We don't. All we know is what Guiying told us. But we know her. I do not think that they will fail.'

His father stayed silent, frowning. At last he nodded. 'The truth is, they are our only hope. They are new to the men, though. I wonder how they will manage.'

'They are your men, Father. They will obey you even in the face of death. You know this.'

The General glanced at him. 'But the tactics are new to me too,' he said quietly. 'And I have to execute the orders.'

Zongbao said, 'Guiying knows them. She will guide us.'

His father began to pace up and down the room in agitation. 'Listen to me,' he said. 'We must talk about the bandit's daughter.'

'What about her?'

He hesitated. 'She bewilders me. She's a martial arts genius, I see that. And that she has – how shall

I say? – a personality of extraordinary force. She is altogether…' He searched for the right word.

'Unusual,' Zongbao said.

The General shot him a look. 'Just so.' He glanced around the darkened room and grunted. 'It would not surprise me to find her here now, having entered the room unnoticed, listening in the corner while I talk about her. In fact, I posted extra guards tonight to make sure that didn't happen. But listen to me. This is our problem: she has never commanded an army. She has never been in a battle before. The men are uneasy, it is only natural. They think she will bring them bad luck.'

Zongbao said, 'I watched them today. I think they have begun to take some notice of her skills. The big man Lun, in particular.'

'It may be. But will they obey her?'

Zongbao was silent.

The General said, 'That is why I have come to a decision. She must remain away from the fighting.'

'But, Father, you promised—'

'I know what I said. Now I speak of what must be.' Fixing his eyes on his son, he said, 'You must keep your wife safe. She will be the mother of your children.' He put his hand on his son's shoulder. 'Enough of this now. Tomorrow we complete our preparations. Be strong, be careful, be—'

He said no more. A deep booming noise split the night-time hush. Alarmed shouts came from the watchtowers and walls. Running to the window and flinging the shutters aside, they were in time to see a red glow unfurl brightly in a far fold of the mountains to the north.

'A huge explosion,' Zongbao said in horror. 'From the direction of Nankou Village.'

His father narrowed his eyes as he stared into the distance. 'It *is* Nankou,' he replied. 'The Liao are already there.'

Turning together, they had a second surprise. Guiying stood in the middle of the room already dressed in body armour, her helmet under her arm.

'Reporting for duty, General sir.' She bowed her head. 'Taking my place at your side,' she added softly, 'as agreed.'

The General swallowed his astonishment and forced his features into an impassive mask. 'Summon the men,' he said firmly. 'All of them. We march through the night.'

16

NIGHT MARCH TO WAR

They set off at second watch. The night sky was turbulent with bulging clouds, the wind sharp with the threat of snow. Six columns of soldiers – ten thousand men – passed out of the gates of Daixian Town and turned north, first the heavy cavalry, next the crossbowmen, then the infantry, the horse-riding infantry, the cavalry wings and finally the rearguard, weighed down with equipment as usual. Except for the creaking of supply wagons and the clatter of horses' hooves, they were silent; and soon they were swallowed up in the darkness of the valley above the town.

There were several villages on the way. Passing through the first of them, they ascended the cliffs on the eastern side of the river and went along the high stony edge of fields planted with sesame, invisible now in the darkness but whispering in the wind.

South of the second village, as the gongsmen sounded third watch, they descended again to the valley and crossed the freezing river at the ford, hurrying northwards as before, a great winding train of men and horses black against the pale cliffs that rose in pleated folds around them. From time to time the captains looked up to the darkness of the mountains above to check the torches of the scouts flickering like distant fireflies among the trees on the ridge, and urged the men on.

Zongbao was at Guiying's side in the vanguard. She rode like a peasant, he noticed, without saddle or stirrups, swaying rhythmically as if she were a part of the horse itself.

'We will be there by noon,' he said. He glanced at her. 'Listen to me. It's possible that in the fight ahead I will die. I want you to know that I will die happy to have been your husband.'

She reached out and touched his hand. 'But I do not think you will die. Nor me,' she said with a smile.

He went on, 'What I want to say is this. If I die, our troops might still succeed. Without *you*, though... the counter-measure will not work. For this reason, forgive me, I think it best for you to stay with the rearguard when the fight begins.'

'So you agreed with your father.'

Zongbao gave her a look. 'Not exactly. But there is sense in what he says. And... and I do not want you to die.'

Before she could reply a summons arrived – Captain Yang to attend the General – and he touched his spurs to his horse and galloped ahead; and she rode on alone, thinking. She thought of her husband, so brave and caring. And of the General, so sensible and dutiful. She thought too of her own duty and where it lay. But most of all she thought of her father, the fat old bandit with the red face; and it came to her that when the battle started she would honour him more than anyone simply by being herself and fighting as he had taught her. It was a curious thought, but it pleased her, and she rode on again with a lighter heart.

The hours passed. Fourth watch – the deepest, darkest hour of the night – came and went. At fifth watch a little green light leaked into the sky from the east and the misty mountainsides came into view, steep cascades of pine forests and rocky outcrops bald as vultures. Above the trees floated the thin signal trails of smoke from the scouts' torches as they went ahead. With great effort the men kept up their pace, and at sunrise they finally entered the ravine that leads to the valley head.

They were only a few hours from Nankou Village now. Again the commanders urged them on.

At the back of the column of infantry, Ying, Ju and Lun marched together in weary silence. They wore the usual body armour of foot soldiers, fish-scales of Chinese paper folded and pressed so many times they had the hardness of iron, and helmets of seasoned black leather. They also carried halberds – long, pronged spears – and the short butterfly swords used by the common soldier for close fighting, while slung over their backs were round wooden shields, scuffed and chipped. Lun towered above the other two, loping along out of step. Several times already he had been rebuked for his slovenly gait and grumpy comments. He was hungry and even more bad-tempered than before.

'By the time we reach Nankou I'm really going to be ready to punch someone,' he muttered to Ying. 'Maybe a commander.'

He was overheard again. To his disgust one of the commanders came alongside, a slender figure hardly bigger than a boy, and as he looked up sullenly, expecting another reprimand, he recognized her at once and moved slightly away, watching her warily. But she said nothing, merely held his gaze for a moment, then touched her helmet with a finger, as if respectfully, and trotted on. After that, he spoke no more about commanders but thought with impatience of the battle to come.

They marched now under a cold blue morning

sky. Ahead of them the ravine twisted north-east, and a little before noon the vanguard led the army along the plain round the curve of the rocks until the valley head came into view, and there they stopped; the rest of the army came to a slow shuffling halt behind them.

They all stared in silence.

Above them in the gorge was a scattered pile of black rubbish, a smudge of smoke. Nothing else. Nankou Village no longer existed. It had been burned to the ground and entirely destroyed.

'We come too late,' Zongbao said bitterly.

The General stared at the scene. A muscle twitched in his cheek. 'Nankou is no more,' he said. 'But the question is: where are the Liao?'

At his side Guiying cleared her throat, and he turned to her in surprise.

'I thought you were with the rearguard,' he said.

She made no reply but pointed over his shoulder towards the high clifftops above them. 'What has happened to the scouts' lanterns?' she said.

They looked up, frowning. The smoke trails had disappeared.

'Listen,' she said.

From the plain came a low rumble growing louder, and, turning on their horses to look down the valley behind them, they saw a gradual trickle of dark forms seeping into view from both sides of the ravine, men jogging with banners, creaking wagons of artillery and endless troops of cavalry, tens of thousands of horsemen galloping into position across the plain, cutting off all retreat.

'We have found the Liao,' Guiying said. 'We did not have to search long.'

'So many,' Zongbao said in awe.

The General rose slightly in his saddle. 'So many who deserve punishment. The children of Nankou will not be forgotten. Now the hard and mighty shall lie beneath the ground.'

Guiying was scanning the lie of the land. 'A good place to fight,' she said, smiling. 'See how they are lining up. Horsemen in front. Crossbowmen on the left wing. Longbowmen on the right. We will answer them with the counter-measure. General,' she said, 'we await your orders.'

He nodded. 'So it begins. Watch their formations. And look for a man on a white horse. It is Xiao Dalin, their general, a man of exceptional ability.'

He gave instructions to his commanders of the crossbowmen, the infantry, the winged-tiger foot soldiers. 'Captain,' he said.

'Yes, sir?' Zongbao said.

'Prepare the heavy cavalry. You will lead the way. And you,' the General said to Guiying.

'Sir?'

'You stay by my side. Today we fight together.'

17

GREAT BEAR AND RED BIRD

There was, as always, the moment of stillness before the chaos of battle; across the plain massed ranks of soldiers silently regarded each other with hatred and fear. With the other winged-tiger infantrymen, Ying, Ju and Lun stood together, gazing towards the Liao army.

'They'll come from the right,' Ying said.

Ju nodded. 'And from the left.'

'Horsemen.'

'Then more horsemen.'

'And horsemen after that.'

They both said together, 'God help us.'

Lun had said nothing.

'Big man?' Ying prompted him.

He did not take his eyes from the Liao army. He was muttering to himself. 'What they have done I will avenge.'

'What?'

'She told me, that devil of a girl. She foresaw it. What they have done I will avenge. Me, Lun. And what have they done? They've killed the kids of Nankou.' He stared fiercely ahead of him. '*So bring them to me!*' he roared.

And at that moment the trumpets sounded, the drums began to beat, and the men surged forward with a tremendous outpouring of noise.

The plain was a natural battle arena, dry and flat. To the east were the mountains, to the west the river, to the north the valley head, to the south the rocky bend in the ravine. There was no escape.

As Ying and Ju had predicted, the Liao horsemen charged first, from both left and right. They hit the two wings of Chinese cavalry hard and wheeled away, swapping flanks, and hit them again from different directions. Before the Chinese could regroup they had swooped away, and the Liao longbowmen ran forward in their place, sending waves of fire-tipped arrows into the Chinese reserve cavalry. At the same time, the Liao crossbowmen advanced unexpectedly from the west, firing volley after volley of bolts into the right flank of the Chinese infantry. The rapid fluidity of the Liao army's transformations was incredible, like a creature constantly changing its shape – now a dragon, now a tiger, now an eagle.

Everything was accompanied by the screams and roars of dying men.

In the Liao command centre, in the heart of their army, a man sat on a stationary white horse, very still, quietly issuing commands to his messengers.

In the Chinese command centre, named Great Bear Constellation, with Guiying at his side the General issued his own orders with trumpet and drum, desperately trying to counter the Liao's swift attacks. His banners moved across the field of battle – Red Bird, Green Dragon and White Tiger – and gradually the Chinese divisions began to block the Liao's thrusts.

In a sandy field bordering the river Zongbao, riding at the head of his men, crashed into the right wing of the oncoming Liao infantry with their halberds and spiked shields, and began to hack his way through their line.

'To me!' he shouted over the din. 'Break them up! Push them back!'

His sword flashed as his horse plunged and reared. Behind him, buffeted in the commotion, his banner of the Red Bird swung wildly.

'To me!' Zongbao called again, and as the flagman fell he caught hold of the banner and held it aloft, his horse leaping high as the Liao stormed around him. He shouted out a third time; and the Liao foot-soldiers were swept away by his cavalry crashing past.

On his dancing horse Zongbao wiped the sweat from his face, looking round anxiously.

'We are holding them,' he said to himself. 'But they are so many. So many.' Scanning the battlefield for further instructions, he heard the drumbeat from Great Bear, and called at once to his men, 'To the left flank! No time to rest! The Liao ride against our bowmen.'

And they were gone from the field, leaving behind a fog of dust and the scattered humps of fallen bodies.

In the very centre of the battleground there was no room for tactics or formations, only the slam and crunch of hand-to-hand fighting, the screams of the wounded and the raw bravery of those still alive. They were packed so close together that the dead often remained upright, wedged between the struggling men.

Inseparable, Ying, Ju and Lun fought together, Lun looming above the rest, laying about him, Ju solidly guarding his back, Ying nimbly covering his weaker left-hand side.

Every few minutes Lun let out a roar. 'For the children!' The Liao who got close to him were clubbed to the ground or slashed by his sword, or picked up bodily and flung away like so many handfuls of clothes. Ying and Ju worked tirelessly to fend off the others.

Yet as the hours passed, they grew tired. Their arms ached, their hands were numb. And they saw that despite their efforts the Liao continued to surge around them in ever greater numbers.

'Ying!' Ju called.

'What is it?'

'I can't go on much longer!'

'Neither can I!'

But Lun shouted, 'Keep them coming! There are still many more children to avenge!'

So, taking heart, they battled on as well they could.

In the small protected enclave of the Great Bear, the General surveyed the battlefield with his spyglass, seeking patterns in the general confusion of men and horses.

'We have been holding them,' he said. 'The counter-measure has worked so far. But we are too few. Green Dragon is falling back. Red Bird is trapped against the cliff-face. Only White Tiger is free. But the men there are tired; they cannot go on much longer.'

Guiying nodded. 'It is time to change our tactics.'

'How?'

She pointed. 'See where they are strongest?'

'Yes.'

'That is where they do not expect us to attack.'

18

OUTNUMBERED

In the shadows of the cliffs the remaining hundred men of the elite Chinese cavalry fought on. They were heavily outnumbered. Zongbao had changed his horse twice and lost his helmet but still he urged his troops forward, though the Liao horsemen harried them hard. The Red Bird banner was still aloft but ripped to shreds. Zongbao could no longer see Great Bear through the smoke nor hear the drum over the crash and yell of the fight.

He was exhausted, and he saw exhaustion in the faces of his men too as they looked to him for guidance.

'Men of China!' he shouted above the din. 'Listen to me!' He wheeled round on his horse, looking at them intently. 'I see the tiredness in your faces. I'm tired myself. But look into the faces of the Liao. There you will see fear. They expected to beat us. But we are not beaten. And today we do not lose!'

His men raised a cheer, but he knew, even before the cheer died away, that they needed something new or – slowly, steadily – they would eventually fall before the Liao's superior numbers.

'Sir!' his lieutenant cried in surprise, pointing towards the enemy.

There was a commotion in the Liao right flank, horses rearing apart left and right as a rogue horseman came riding at speed, weaving swiftly through their ranks towards Zongbao.

A horseman without a saddle, no bigger than a boy.

She cantered gracefully up to him, reined in her horse and saluted.

'Guiying! What are you doing here?'

'Your father sends his greetings. We have suffered terrible losses. We are falling back everywhere. The men are exhausted, they cannot go on.' She smiled. 'So. Now it is time for us to win.'

'Easier said than done.'

'Of course. But also harder to think than to do. We have already thought how to do it, so the hard part is out of the way. We will attack their centre of command at once.'

'Where their defences are strongest?'

'Exactly.'

His heart leaped inside him. 'I am with you.'

She smiled again. 'Shall we go then, together?'

He stood up in his stirrups and called to his remaining comrades. 'Men of China! Remember what I have told you. Today they cannot beat us. And now it is time for us to seize the victory. To me! To me! For the Emperor, for China and for the children of Nankou!'

And, finding energy from somewhere, they turned as one and streamed in spearhead formation against the unwary Liao who scattered before them.

In Great Bear, the still centre of the continuing chaos, gazing steadfastly through his spyglass, the General saw the change at once. He gave the orders to reinforce the new attack. Green Dragon turned inwards from the river edge and broke through the Liao western defences. The Chinese bowmen swung round to fix their sights on the new target and rained their arrows on the Liao command. The winged-tiger infantrymen, sensing the sudden shift in their fortunes and eager not to be left out, caught hold of the stirrups of the Red Bird horsemen as they galloped past and were carried into the thick of the fighting with them. The Liao imploded at the centre and their men scattered outwards.

* * *

On a shallow rise of grass where, an hour before, Xiao Dalin – the General of the Great Liao – had sat on his white horse issuing his orders, Guiying and Zongbao rested now, getting back their breath, watching the aftermath of the fighting around them, rearguard actions as the Liao troops fled the field, leaving behind the many dead.

'We took them by surprise,' Zongbao said. 'They could not imagine we would attempt such a thing.'

Guiying said, 'Failure of the imagination is always the worst fault in a battle. And in life,' she added, 'for if we do not imagine the things we want to do we will not attempt them. But look,' she said, 'you are wounded.'

Zongbao looked down. His sleeve was soaked in blood. 'It is nothing. There are men who have suffered far worse.'

They gazed about them again, at the skirmishes that continued as the Liao fought to escape.

'We have too few men to hunt them down,' Zongbao said. 'They will regroup and attack again.'

She made no reply, scanning the battlefield keenly, peering through the dust and smoke.

'But now we have a chance to rest,' he said. 'At least for a little while. Guiying?'

He turned to look for her. But she was no longer there.

* * *

There was one place on the battlefield where the men did not know that the battle was over: in the centre, where the common soldiers fought to the death. The men here had little chance to notice anything but the blur and stab of axe and sword.

And in the very centre of the centre, one man fought alone against the Liao troops who crowded round him. A huge man battered now almost beyond recognition. He had no companions any more; they lay at his feet crumpled together. His face was bloodied. His left arm was paralysed, his sword was long gone, his shield too. But Lun continued to punch and chop and kick with sullen determination, muttering to himself something about children.

He was going to die, he had no doubt about that. But he would die having fulfilled a minor prophecy, for he had avenged the lost children of Nankou.

There was a lull around him as the Liao regrouped. They knew he was finished; they gathered themselves now for a last murderous rush. Swaying, he steadied himself, wiping the blood from his eyes, preparing himself for the end. Then they came at him, all together, knives out.

And were swept away in a confusion of arms and legs by a horseman arriving out of nowhere. Lun looked about him, bewildered. The horse reared above him, riderless.

'Saved by a horse!?' he exclaimed.

Guiying landed lightly next to him. 'Come,' she said. 'It is time to quit this brawling. The General has summoned you.'

Lun scowled. 'Another punishment?'

She smiled. 'He wishes to thank you in person. The battle is won and vengeance is yours. See what you have done.'

He turned, and to his surprise saw that the Liao had fled. He looked down at his feet. 'But… my friends,' he said in a broken voice.

'More heroes. We will honour them too. But come,' Guiying said gently. 'You must not keep the General waiting.'

There was nothing left around them but smoke and the hush of death. The first of the crows came down from the sky. And Guiying and Lun went slowly from the field, together.

19

THE ATTACK AT YUKOU DITCH

There was no time for celebration. They buried their dead, evacuated the low-lying villages, and within three days had returned to the fortress of Daixian. There the weeks passed in renewed training for, as Zongbao had foreseen, the Liao were preparing to attack again – scouts sent reports of more horsemen massing in the valleys to the north and east. Occasionally there were skirmishes with bands of their cavalry, sometimes within sight of the town's walls.

In the General's study, they discussed what to do. Lun, who had become the General's personal bodyguard, watched the door.

'This is our ground,' the General said. 'It favours us

as they do not know it. But we are still too weak. We need more men.'

'Will we get reinforcements?' Guiying asked.

'I await word from the Imperial adviser, Fu Xian.'

Zongbao was more upbeat. 'We were outnumbered before but we beat them anyway.'

His father said, 'The Liao have built up their army since then. There is a rumour that the Empress Dowager is to join them. At Nankou we drove them from the battlefield. But when we next engage we must drive them all the way out of China. For that we must be stronger.'

'But, Father—'

'Your courage does you credit. But remember, we still don't have the full counter-measure. We must wait to hear what Fu Xian can do for us.'

So they waited. And after five more days they heard from him.

'What does he say?' Zongbao asked impatiently.

His father passed him the message with a grim expression. 'He expresses disappointment that we have been so careless as to lose so many men, and advises us to avoid bothering the Emperor with such trivial requests again.'

'In that case there is no reason to delay. We must attack the Liao at once,' Zongbao said angrily.

'It is not so simple.'

They argued long into the night.

'Guiying,' Zongbao said, 'tell my father that we will be successful. The Liao do not expect us to take the fight to them. We can surprise them.'

All this time she had listened to them argue, saying nothing. Now, at last asked her opinion, she thought for a moment. 'I do not doubt that we can take them by surprise. But I ask myself one thing.'

'What is it?'

'The Empress Dowager. What surprise will she bring on their side?'

Zongbao frowned. 'I don't understand. She is not a commander.'

'She is the difference. Last time she was not with them; this time she is.'

'I am sure they will fight the same way, with the Heavenly Gate.' He turned to his father. 'If we do not fight now, they will only grow stronger, and soon they will be ready to lay siege to Daixian Town. They are already building the engines.'

The General nodded. 'That is true.' He turned to Guiying. 'I fear we must do something.'

She bowed her head. 'Very good. I will study our options.'

The General nodded. 'In the meantime we do not underestimate the enemy. We must strengthen our walls, organize our defences, even plan what to do in the event of a defeat. The example of Nankou is clear. To fight on we must survive.'

* * *

Next morning a scout brought news. By chance, a cousin of his living in the mountains to the south had told him of strangers gathered at Yukou, by the great ditch, a day's ride away. He had been to see for himself. They were Liao.

'So far south?' Zongbao said in surprise. 'How many?'

Only a handful, the man said. It was not a military gathering but, more likely, a secret meeting of leaders, a brief conference before operations began. There was a man who rode a white horse attended by many guards, others too of high rank. Their horses and uniforms were splendid. The scout had even seen a sedan chair, red-lacquered and finely carved with a white banner hoisted above it.

'The chair of the Empress Dowager,' the General said. 'So it is true: she has arrived. She will be conferring with Xiao Dalin and her other generals. But why so far south? What interests them there?'

They questioned the scout but he could give them no further answers.

When he had gone, Zongbao was unable to contain his excitement. 'You see what this means? All their leaders gathered in one place. With one blow we can cut off the army's head. We have no need for great numbers. Only a few dozen men, travelling fast.' He turned to Guiying. 'This is our opportunity.'

'And our danger,' said the General.

'What's wrong with danger when there is so great a prize?'

The General was thoughtful. 'The prize is great indeed.'

Zongbao turned to Guiying. 'What do you say? Shall I go?'

She thought for a moment. 'On one condition.'

'What is that?'

'You take me with you.'

He hesitated, but only for a moment. 'If I have learned anything, it is how hard it is to stop you doing what you want to do.'

'Very well,' the General said. 'Pick your men. Leave before dawn.' He paused. 'And return safely, both of you.'

It was still dark when they left, riding swiftly through swirling snow along the road towards the green-tinged rise of mountains beyond. Passing the last village at noon, they climbed steeply through forest to the summit and went on again, faster, along the winding ridge. To the south-west the green hills fell in vast, crinkled swathes towards the Imperial capital of Bianjing in the far distance; to the north and east the bare mountains rose higher to wildernesses inhabited only by panthers and eagles.

Early in the afternoon the scout led them down off the ridge into woodland and they went on in silence, using only hand signals to communicate with each other. Descending into a ravine, they went slowly up the far side on a goat trail and dismounted in a grove of holm oaks about two kilometres from their destination. There they separated, climbing the rest of the way on foot, meeting again an hour later at the summit, where they lay under a shelf of rock, looking down.

Below was the Yukou Ditch, part of the defences built hundreds of years earlier against the horsemen; and camped on the shallow plain next to the ditch were half a dozen tents of black hemp. Smoke rose lazily from them. Liao troops were stationed outside the tents and round the perimeter.

It was just as the scout had said.

They conferred in whispers.

'They will have posted lookouts in the woods below,' Zongbao said.

Guiying nodded. 'There were five. Unusually careless. They aren't looking out any more.'

He looked at her in amazement.

'This is my sort of country,' she added simply.

Business-like, the captain glanced up at the sky. 'Twilight is the best time to move. Light enough for us to see them, shadowy enough for us to conceal ourselves.'

'One hour,' she said.

It was agreed.

* * *

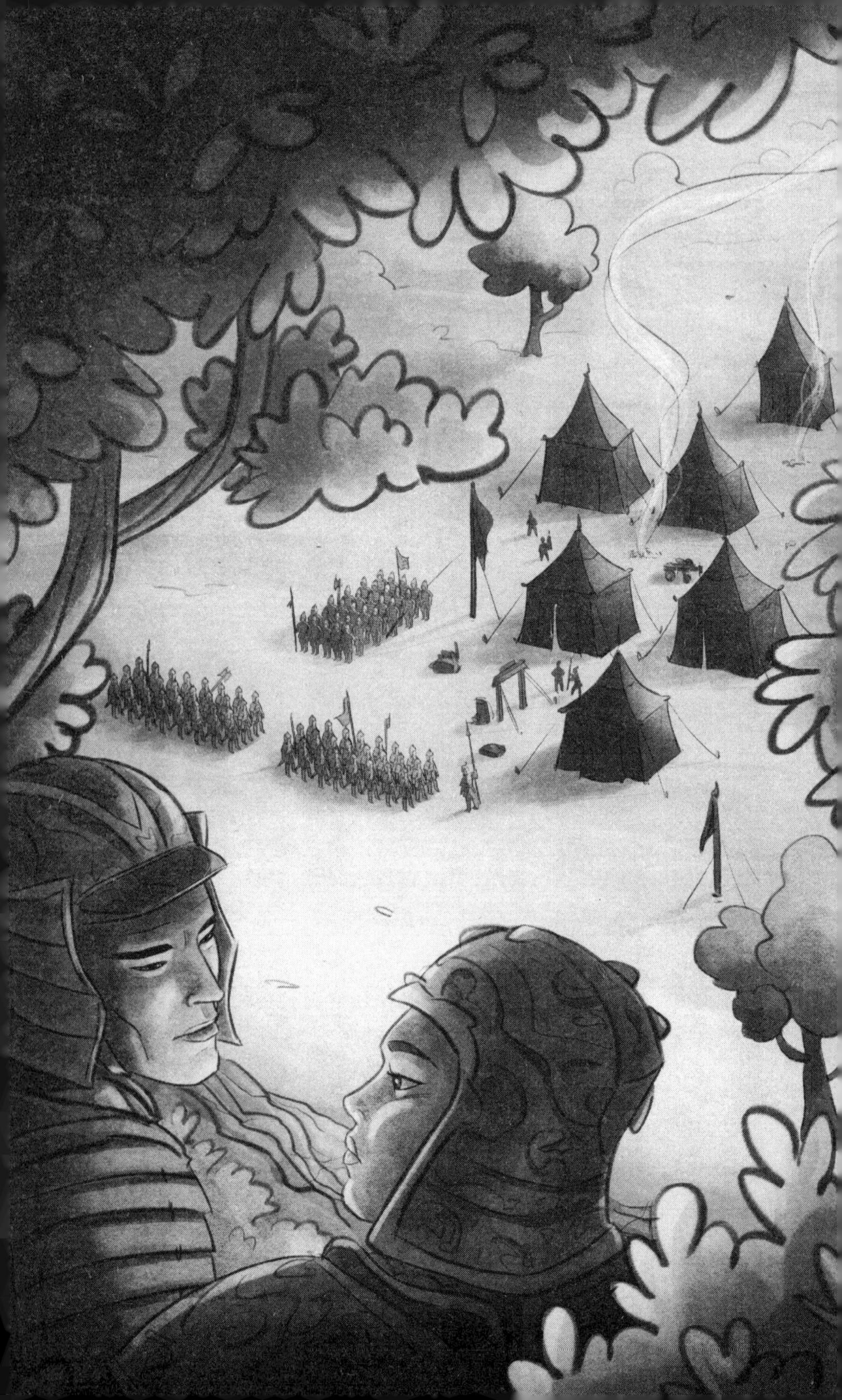

A birdcall was the signal to begin it. They went from tree to tree down the slope, shadows among the shadows, and came to the plain below without the alarm being raised. Everything was quiet. Nothing stirred except the quietly flickering glow of braziers inside the tents.

Zongbao led a band of men under cover towards the wagons beyond the tents, where the Liao guards had their shelter. Guiying went stealthily the other way towards the sentries along the Ditch. Another birdcall sent them into action. Shadows leaped. There were muffled cries strangled immediately to silence.

In the stillness they watched for signs of movement. There was none. And now at last they broke cover and went at speed across the open plain, running fast and low, feet thumping on the dry earth, knives out. The Liao guarding the tent entrances rushed forward with cries of alarm to confront the attackers, but they were soon overpowered; moments later Zongbao and his men crashed into the tents.

And found them empty.

They knew at once how bad their mistake had been. Grouped again outside, panting, peering around as they stood back to back, they could only watch as the horsemen came silently out of the shadows and circled the little plain, many hundreds of them. Not all of them were Liao. Many wore strange uniforms which Guiying recognized after a moment as belonging to the Western Xia, old friends of the Liao. One rider – a short, broad man with a wizened face – sat on a white horse, staring at them blankly.

It was a trap.

The Chinese scout fell to his knees in front of Zongbao. 'Forgive me,' he cried. 'They said they would kill my family.'

For several minutes the horsemen made no move. Then, at last, their horses parted and a red-lacquered sedan chair was brought into view. Out of it stepped a tiny old woman in a gold costume. She said nothing. Her face was expressionless. For a long moment she simply stared at the Chinese; then she lifted something into the air and smiled.

It was the mummified head of Zongbao's grandfather, Yang Ye!

Zongbao could not help himself. 'No!' Guiying cried, but for once she was too late. As Zongbao leaped towards the Empress Dowager the air around him shrieked and he fell in a sprawl, riddled with arrows.

Then the horsemen rushed in from all sides.

20

ALONE

In the desolate mountains south of the Yukou Ditch there is nothing but trees and rock and streams. The eagles soaring day after day over forests and peaks never catch sight of a human being. At night the frozen silence of the vast slopes is as thick as the darkness of the sky above. Nothing stirs.

But tonight, the second night after the slaughter at Yukou, the silence was broken by the light pattering of bare feet. A girl running between the trees. Slowly, in pain, going on goat trails through forests, down ravines, along ridges, making her way step by step towards the great river valley to the north. Every few hours she stopped and gazed up at the stars to check her position and drank a little water from a stream. She washed her wounds and loosened the belt of her tunic, then ran on again.

As she ran she thought carefully about what had come to pass, and what was to come. Images came into her mind: Zongbao sprawling in the dirt, the Empress grinning, the horsemen surging forward. She saw again the butchery in the twilight, the explosive tracery of arrows, the glittering dance of swords. Saw the men who came against her, their eagerness and stupidity, the shapes they made as they fell. And she felt again the pain of knowing she must leave behind the body of her husband for his enemies. She had stayed fighting for too long indeed, and had the wounds to prove it, but at last, in the confusion, she had slipped away. Only three or four men noticed her go and soon, when she got them among the trees, they noticed no more.

Alone on the summit above the Ditch she had paused to look down one last time at the horsemen idling now around the pile of bodies, Zongbao's among them.

She knew now what difference the Empress Dowager had brought to the Liao: an alliance with the Western Xia – the sight of their horsemen had told her as much. She must warn the Chinese that they were facing a much bigger army. And she had another duty, far more painful. To tell the General that his only son was dead.

With a last look at the scene below, she had turned and begun to run steadily, into the wind.

As she went, she had time to reflect on herself too. Her husband was dead and she was alone. In truth she had always felt alone, but now she was bereft, and in her misery she thought of her father, the fat old bandit. He had not been a good father, but his harshness had taught her one thing. To be herself. It gave her some comfort, even in her misery, to know that she remained who she was.

By noon on the third day she reached a small village at the western end of the mountain range, and there persuaded the blacksmith to lend her a horse. She rode down to the plain and galloped towards Daixian Town.

When she was still five kilometres away, as night began to fall, she saw a red glow on the horizon ahead, and her heart sank as she quickened her pace. At the last village on the southern side of the river she could hear the explosions in the distance. And when she finally reached the river and reined in her horse, it was to watch Daixian Town burn.

She was too late. The town had been overrun by a huge army of Liao and Western Xia, their forces even now stretching far to the east along the valley.

There was no time to rest. She could not delay. Turning her horse, she rode hard to the west along the south bank of the river searching across the water until finally – three hours later – she found what she had hoped to find. In the darkness they were hard to see, but her eyes were keen: a small flotilla of river boats with slatted woven sails gliding silently along without lights.

Sliding off her horse as it cantered on, Guiying ran to the water's edge and dived lightly in.

Standing on the prow of the leading boat, two men stood talking in low voices. One voice was stern and commanding, clipped with the strain of self-control; the other was blunt and coarse.

'How many men?' the first voice asked sharply.

'Not enough,' snarled the second. 'Most are dead.'

There was a pause.

'Horses?'

'Half as many as we need.'

'Weapons?'

'No point in asking. Better get used to kicking and punching.'

'I am used to it.'

A grunt.

'What, Lun?'

'That arm of yours. Ought to get it looked at now.'

'The surgeons will still be busy with the civilians. I can wait.'

Another grunt. Silence fell. The boat sped noiselessly through the darkness.

After a while the first voice spoke again. 'What was that noise?'

'Didn't hear nothing. A fish.'

'I want total silence on this boat till we are well away from pursuit. Go and see to it, Lun.'

Lumbering footsteps went aft, leaving the first man standing alone in the darkness. Everything was still and quiet. After a moment, without changing his position, he said in a low even voice, 'I know you're there. Come out where I can see you.'

Still there was no movement.

He went on in the same voice, 'After what's happened, you might be thinking I'm tired enough, or weak enough, for you to take me. I tell you this, whoever you are, Daixian Town may have fallen. But I have not. Come out and I will show you how weak I am.'

At last a shadow detached itself from the shadow of the low sail, stepped forward and stood there with bowed head.

For a long moment the General looked at her steadily.

'Where is my son?'

She made no reply. A single tear ran down her cheek.

He said nothing. His expression did not change. As he turned to go, he put his hand on her shoulder briefly, then went in his usual unbending fashion along the deck to his cabin.

* * *

In the days that followed, Guiying and the General spoke little. He asked her only once to tell him what happened at the Yukou Ditch, then spoke of it no more. He did not blame her but she felt his silent anger. Briefly he described to her the overwhelming assault on Daixian Town, his decision to evacuate and continue the fight elsewhere.

'We will never give up.'

'The Emperor?'

'My messages have been returned unread.' He gestured southwards. 'Many li ahead of us is Changyuan, the last fortress this side of the Yellow River. There we will make our final stand. If we get there,' he added. 'We have a long way to go, and the enemy will be close behind.'

He was right. They were sorely harried by both the Liao and the Western Xia as they fled south along the great rivers. At the gap in the mountains north of the Tea Horse Road, they were bombarded by Liao giant crossbows set high on the ridges, and lost two of their boats. Five days later the men of the Western Xia came down suddenly off the plateau and destroyed another with a firestorm. For many days, in the shadows of the giant statues of Buddha that line the ancient route, they fought their way through earthquake country north of the Yellow River. And after three weeks, they arrived at Changyuan, exhausted but alive.

The General looked back along the river. 'Such a long way they have they pursued us, thinking to destroy us entirely. But there is fight left in us, they will see.' He stepped from the boat with Guiying at his side and looked up at the city walls. 'Here it will happen,' he said. 'We have no reason to be afraid, for if we die we honour my son, who died for us.'

She said, 'But if we live we can avenge his death.'

He did not look at her but went on alone through the gates into the city.

21

UNDER SIEGE

They hoped they might have a week in which to prepare. They had a day. At nightfall the torches of the horsemen appeared on the plain to the north.

Summoned to the General's rooms, Guiying found him performing a private rite. Dressed in a long cotton tunic of white, the colour of death, he was kneeling at a shallow white porcelain bowl burning squares of golden metallic joss paper printed with red rectangles, the ghost money of lost soldiers.

He rose to face her. He said, 'Custom forbids me from offering my prayers, for the elder can never give respect to the younger, but at least now my son has money for the afterlife.'

'I am younger than he was,' she replied softly, 'and I have not stopped praying.'

The General said nothing to that and she felt his grief. She felt something else too: a sense of her own failure. The General had not blamed her for Zongbao's death, but there were times when she sensed the unspoken anger in him. After all, she had returned alive and Zongbao had not returned at all. She would not be surprised if the General decided to dismiss her from his service.

Indeed he turned to her now with a severe expression. 'I have something else to say to you.'

'Sir.'

'You may find this hard.'

She bowed her head and waited.

'I wish you to take my son's position. To lead our men in the field as our commander.'

She stared at him in surprise.

'I have today heard from Fu Xian. I have roused the Emperor to great anger, it seems, with my failures. So there is no doubt: we are alone. The men have seen you fight and will obey you.' He hesitated. 'These are not the only reasons, however.'

His expression did not change, though his face seemed to stiffen.

'My son loved you. I have heard what you said: by fighting you will avenge him. I give you this opportunity. I know you will not fail.'

*   *   *

The siege began. The month of the ox gave way to the month of the tiger, with snow in the air at dawn and sleet through the night, and the long, wide plain around the city slowly blackened with the camped armies of the Liao and Western Xia. Behind their tents, where furnace fires burned all night, they built their siege towers, catapults and rams; every week their ships brought more men and equipment.

Directed by the Liao general Xiao Dalin, always on his white horse, they began their assaults. They drove their falcon carts up against the low-lying eastern walls and tore down the wooden palings with their great hooks. They bombarded the watchtowers with their slingshots. They heaved their scaling ladders against the western walls and fought their way as far as the parapets. They gave the defenders no rest.

The Chinese stubbornly persisted.

Food ran scarce; people ate their household pets.

The walls were damaged; gangs of men and women worked all night to repair them, dismantling their houses to plug the cracks and holes with parts of doors and window frames.

The attackers scaled the southern ramparts with grappling hooks; the soldiers poured water down the walls, turning them to curtains of unclimbable ice. Though they now numbered no more than five thousand, the defenders kept to their stations, repelling the enemy's furious assaults.

But in the long hours of the night, watched over by Lun, Guiying and the General found it hard to keep their hopes alive.

'Even the counter-measure would not help us now,' the General said. 'We are too few. Anyway, it isn't complete. We have always lacked the final part.'

Guiying thought about that. She said, 'When my father was drunk he would sometimes joke with me. He had a saying he liked very much: "the final part of the puzzle is the puzzle".'

Lun said, 'Yeah, that sounds like someone who's drunk.'

She ignored him. 'Then he would say, "So, you see, it isn't like the other parts."'

The General looked at her. 'What did he mean?'

'I think of it this way. The final part changes all the other parts. Only with the final part does the puzzle become itself.'

'Still sounds a bit drunk to me,' Lun said.

It was late. They turned to other matters, the worrying build-up of horsemen on the southern plain, a possible assault by the siege engines positioned to the west.

'They have overwhelming force,' the General said. 'Soon they will discover how to use it. We must constantly guard against it.'

Guiying was thoughtful. 'Unless…'

'What?'

Her face was grave. 'We are not the only ones looking for the final part of a puzzle. So too are they. Suppose their final part is not overwhelming force – but something different.'

The General considered this. 'You think they will try something new?'

She did not have the chance to answer. The night-time hush was abruptly shattered by bells ringing out urgently. Shouts came from the surrounding buildings. There were running feet in the corridor outside and the door burst open.

'Sir! Riders!'

'Where?'

'In the compound!'

'*In the compound?*' They were all instantly on their feet. 'How did they get through the gates?'

The men did not know. But, somehow, several hundred horsemen had found their way inside the city's defences.

Guiying said, 'Something new, as you say. Perhaps this is the final piece of their puzzle.'

'They can be as different as they like,' the General said, taking his sword down from the wall. 'We fight them just the same.'

They ran together from the room – into a hubbub of panic and confusion. Soldiers roused from their bivouacs were hurrying in different directions putting on their armour. Women and children were fleeing to the temple. Nothing could be heard above the clamour of bells and horns, the roar of shouts and oaths, nothing made sense in the chaotic blur of torchlight and shadows.

But a much stranger sight awaited them. Dashing at last into the compound, expecting to be in the thick of the fighting, they found themselves in a surreal scene of inexplicable stillness, and came to a halt, staring round bewildered. Strange horsemen, many hundreds of them, stood in silent stationary ranks behind a single closed carriage. Stranger still, the Chinese soldiers who had reached the compound before them had thrown down their weapons, and now lay on the ground in submission.

As they watched, the carriage door was opened and a stern-faced figure in a long red robe and square black hat appeared.

The blood drained from the General's face.

It was the Emperor.

22

THE EMPEROR'S COMMANDS

Imperial troops ran forward, displacing the General's men, and formed a guard of honour. Flagmen took up positions behind them with banners of Song purple and red flame, and buglers sounded a long, shrill fanfare as the Emperor descended from his carriage.

He was a fat man with a sallow face from which hung a drooping moustache and a wispy chin beard; his eyes were small and shrewd, glancing about him as he came across the compound with small deliberate steps.

Silence was total as he reached the little group. With an imperious gesture he commanded them to rise, and they obeyed, Lun scowling, occasionally opening his mouth and shutting it again, the General upright and blank-faced, Guiying at ease as usual.

For a moment the Emperor looked at her with his narrow, unblinking eyes, as if noting her for later, then he returned his gaze to the General.

'Yang Yanzhou, son of Yang Ye.' His voice was quiet and efficient.

The General bowed his head.

'You are a long way from my northern border.'

The General said nothing. A muscle twitched in his cheek.

'My villages of Fanshi and Nankou are burned to the ground. The fortress of Daixian is destroyed. The long road to Changyuan is littered with defeats. A fleet of my boats is drowned in the rivers, their men lost. And in all these lands of mine, even to the very gates of this city, the Empress Dowager of the Great Liao does exactly what she pleases.' The Emperor paused, though his eyes did not leave the General's face. 'How do you answer?'

Yang Yanzhou swallowed. When he spoke his voice was low and bitter. 'It is as your Excellency says. I will not hide the truth. I will only add that at Yukou the body of my only son lies unburied.'

'Just so.' The Emperor glanced again at Guiying, who held his gaze, and he turned back to the General, speaking more sharply now. 'How many men have you lost?'

'At least ten thousand.'

'How many machines, horses, boats, weapons?'

'Past counting.'

'How many children and women in the villages and towns?'

'More than I know how to grieve.'

'What *do* you know, General?'

He did not hesitate. 'Only how to lay down my life for my country.'

The Emperor looked a long time into the General's face after this. He clapped his hands and Imperial guards ran forward to surround them.

'Behold this man,' he said loudly for all to hear. 'Defender of my northern border, as his father was before him. Look well, and remember what I tell you now.' He paused. 'He is my loyal servant,' he said. 'He fought on alone when my advisers refused to give him aid. He has suffered terrible losses but never once thought of surrender. Behold him now. His hour of need is *my* hour of need. And therefore, General,' he said quietly, 'I am come to join with you in this struggle.'

There was a long moment while they all tried to understand this. Lun made a series of meaningless noises only partially smothered.

'You thought you were disgraced, I see. No. But an Emperor may be disgraced by his advisers. I have been taught a valuable lesson in dishonesty by Fu Xian. He kept from me the truth of your exploits.' He made a quick shape with his hands, suddenly business-like, his eyes keen. 'Come. There is no time to lose. I only learned the facts a few days ago. Now I have seen the situation for myself. Reinforcements are being gathered, a vast army, but they will not arrive for many weeks. All I have brought with me are the Imperial guard and a solitary crossbow machine. And myself, to give a little hope to my people. With these we must survive. What is our plan? What's to be done?'

As the General hesitated, Guiying stepped forward. 'I know.'

The Emperor looked at her astonished. The General and Lun looked at her, astonished too.

She paid no attention to them. She said, 'While you've been talking, I've been thinking. It has come to me. I know how my father would have completed the counter-measure. The last part of the puzzle.'

23

THE FINAL PIECE OF THE PUZZLE

The Emperor said, 'Who was your father? Who are *you*?'

'My father was a rough and bitter man. You knew him as the bandit Mu Yu of the Mu Ke fortress. But before he was sent into exile he was the Emperor's loyal war strategist.'

The Emperor said quietly, 'You speak now of the Emperor my father. I was a boy at court.' He stared at her. 'You are Mu Yu's daughter? A *girl*, here?' He frowned a deep, dangerous frown – then began to laugh, his fat face bunching, his beard dithering below his chin. 'I see you are not usual,' he said at last.

'You are correct,' the General said without meaning to.

'Strangest girl I ever met,' blurted Lun. 'Is she even a girl? More like something dropped from the sky.'

The Emperor looked thoughtfully at Guiying. 'You can break the siege?'

She bowed her head. 'I can defeat the Liao and the Western Xia and drive them from your kingdom.'

'This does not sound easy.'

She smiled. 'The final part of the puzzle is neither easy nor hard. It is only hard to find.'

The Emperor gave a brisk nod. 'I have absolutely no idea what you mean.' He caught the eye of Lun, who was frankly suffering the same problem. 'We await your explanation, the big man and I.'

And, clapping his hands, he went with them through the compound gates towards the General's rooms.

Operations began after nightfall the following day. Under cover of darkness three teams of riders set out in different directions. They rode low and hard onto the plain and were soon swallowed up in the darkness.

From the ramparts Guiying watched them go. 'It is begun. Though the Liao don't know it yet.'

The Emperor, standing next to her, said, 'How long before they do?'

She shrugged. 'Four days, maybe five. But we must be busy now with our other preparations.'

* * *

Two nights later, far away in the distant northern mountains of Taihang, above the narrow gorge known as Two Peaks, a man removed the last wooden chock from a high rock face, and watched with his comrades as the boulders teetered, collided and suddenly plunged together with an enormous dull clatter into the river far below, blocking the narrow channel.

Far to the west in the Mianchi mountains, where the Yellow River squeezes between cliffs, men concealed among the rocks at the water's edge took careful aim with their harpoons and holed the lead junk of the passing convoy below the waterline. As it lurched wildly, snagging on an outcrop, the following junks could not avoid it and their wreckage piled up until the passage was choked with timbers.

North of the city of Anyang, where the ancient north–south road is carried over three major rivers by great stone bridges, a dozen men completed their engineering efforts and retreated to watch the effects. One by one the bridges shifted, warped and finally, with a grating rumble, subsided into the water.

Two days after that, on the plain in front of Changyuan, the Liao's furnaces went out one by one and the work on their siege engines came to a halt. Attacks on the walls of the city slowed, then stopped. Spies reported discontent among the enemy troops, disagreements between the leaders of the armies. Within a week, troops of the Western Xia started to disappear.

'You cut off their supplies,' the Emperor said.

Guiying nodded. 'The General had reminded me that both the Liao and the Western Xia are a long way from home. Their supply routes were too stretched; they must get their food, their equipment, their reinforcements, from far away. Now they cannot get them at all. We have blocked the roads and rivers.' A faint smile came to her lips. 'This was the missing last part of the counter-measure. A new idea that changes everything on the battlefield. They cannot fight so well when they are hungry and short of weapons.'

The Emperor nodded. 'General?'

'Our plans are laid,' the General said. 'We ride out to meet them tomorrow at dawn. We are still outnumbered but we can wait no longer.'

Guiying said, 'Besides, this time we have a secret weapon.'

The Emperor looked interested. 'And what is that?'

She smiled again. 'You,' she said.

24

THE LAST STAND

The winter dawn came late, glittering and cold. Mist lay on the river like breath on a mirror. The gates of Changyuan shunted open with a groan and the army of the Chinese marched onto the field. As the General had said, they were still outnumbered, by as many as five to one, but their soldiers went forward with grim determination to save their city or die in the attempt. They saw at once that it would be one or the other, for the Liao troops moved swiftly to cut off their retreat. On the great plain they were completely surrounded.

Guiying rode at the General's side in her new captain's uniform. Her eyes were on the enemy but her thoughts were for her dead husband. Promoted to his position, she felt out of place at the heart of the army. But only for a moment. It didn't matter what uniform she wore or what title she was given. She was Mu Guiying, bandit's daughter; nothing would change that. And, as she took her place with the General in Great Bear, she gave her attention again to the opposing troops.

'Do you see the white horse?' he asked.

'Not yet.'

'No matter. We must not delay.'

The soldiers waiting around them moved restlessly in their long ranks, their horses stamping and snickering.

She said, 'The men are anxious.'

The General nodded. 'They need something to give them courage and strength. Are we in position?'

She waved once to the rearguard at the back, once to the vanguard at the front, and nodded.

'Then let us give it to them.'

All the flagmen dipped their banners. There was a sudden sort of stillness among the men as if they sensed something unusual was about to happen, and they began craning their necks to look about them. Then there was a small movement in the vanguard that attracted their attention…

A single figure in the back of a chariot stood upright and, as they watched, he lifted off the hood of his cloak and let it fall; and everyone in the Chinese army looked at him.

Everyone in the Liao army too. Surprise froze their faces.

They saw a fat man in a long red robe with a square black hat. He said nothing at all but lifted his hand above his head; and clenched in it was a short butterfly sword, the favoured weapon of the common soldier.

The Chinese roared their approval as they recognized their Emperor standing with them in their hour of danger. Banners rose into the air, drums rolled, bugles sounded, and they surged forward with sudden energy to engage the waiting Liao.

So it began: the rush and crunch of bodies, screams of horses, the screech of arrows, the thud of bolts; and everywhere the outrage of fury and pain. Smoke and dust rose over hurrying men and charging horses.

In Great Bear the General and Guiying issued orders to counter the Liao's ever-changing battle formations.

In the rearguard, having acknowledged her wave, Lun told his men to remove the camouflage cover from the giant crossbow and, together, they bent to haul it into position. To the sound of a drumbeat – and Lun's oaths – they heaved, straining; the great iron wheels turned and the machine moved forward, creaking loudly, the huge square wooden frame swaying above the cart.

'Faster, curse you!' he shouted. 'They're counting

on us. Quickly, before the Liao spot what we're doing.'

As the bent men redoubled their efforts, Lun estimated the distance to the place where they needed to take the crossbow to stand, and judged they would make it in time. Then there was a big blunt noise like the crashing of a sea wave and he found himself on the ground, horses' hooves plunging above him, swords slashing the air. A lance was thrust down at him; he rolled violently aside and scrambled again to his feet.

'The bow!' he shouted. 'The bow!' And was knocked down again from behind.

In Great Bear, the General and Guiying had been joined by the Emperor, who refused to retreat to a place of greater safety. Together, they scanned the battlefield.

The General asked once again, 'Do you see the white horse?'

She looked hard. 'I do not.'

For a long moment he moved the spyglass across the scene in front of him until finally he found what he was looking for.

'I understand,' he said softly. 'Today there is a *black* horse. Good; it is a sign of his fear. Do you see him now?'

She took the spyglass and nodded. 'It is time. Give the signal to Lun. He must be ready for me.' She leaped up onto her horse.

The Emperor put his hand on her bridle. 'Listen to me,' he said. 'Have you considered well? What you are going to do is reckless.'

She nodded. 'Which is why they won't be expecting it.'

'It places you in great danger.'

She gestured around the field. 'We are all in danger now.'

He grunted his agreement. 'How many go with you?'

She smiled. 'Why would we waste men on something so reckless and dangerous? Especially,' she added, 'when a girl can do it on her own.'

Then she was gone, her horse streaking towards the enemy lines, and the General gave the signal to the rearguard.

Lun saw it out of the corner of his eye as he ducked under a sword thrust. He dragged a man off his horse and stamped on his head, then, turning, punched another in the throat. Half of his men were lost already – they lay twisted on the ground – but the beaten Liao wheeled away and the remaining Chinese soldiers hurried to the great crossbow and hauled it forward again, Lun urging them on once more.

'Hurry! We have to make it! Only a few paces!' He winced as he shouted, feeling the wounds beneath his shattered fish-scale armour. For a moment his eyes glazed over with the pain. Then he shouted again, 'Almost there! One more heave!'

He straightened up to look for the second signal, and out of nowhere a crossbow bolt thumped into his shoulder, spinning him round and dumping him on the ground. As he sat there, dazed, seeing nothing, hearing the hot uproar of men dying around him, he thought for a moment he was done for. But he refused to die. He shook his head and cleared his eyes, and slowly hauled himself to his feet.

The giant crossbow, he noticed, was only a step or two from the necessary position. But as he took a step towards it, something heavy struck him dully in the head and he fell again into the dirt.

She went at speed, crouched low over her horse's neck, between groups of startled Liao soldiers, like the shadow of a cloud racing silently across the ground.

A horse reared up against her; she slashed its harness with her butterfly sword as she passed, and changed direction. She swerved again, leaped over a line of infantrymen and accelerated between two troops of cavalry. She was in the thick of the Liao army now, too close for them to fire arrows at her. A horseman appeared suddenly next to her, drawing back his lance; she swayed to the left, swung both legs to the right and punch-kicked him off his horse.

The Emperor was right, she thought. I am reckless.

All the time she kept her eye on the squat figure on the black horse ahead. She could see how closely he was following her movements, angrily directing his men to intercept her.

He sees my recklessness, she thought. But does not yet understand how dangerous I am.

Just then a force of Liao cavalry swung together to block her way, too many to pass. Her horse bucked as she swerved round them, a sword struck her a glancing blow on her helmet – and she fell.

They surrounded her at once, winged-tiger infantrymen with their twirling staves and knives, and there was no time for thought of any kind any more.

Slowly rising to her feet, she drained herself of all thinking. She became pure movement. She became the fight. And she spun forward suddenly in a blur of kicks.

By now their overwhelming numbers had carried the Liao far into the Chinese lines. Counter-measures could no longer parry the rapid thrusts of their army. In Great Bear, the General continued to direct operations, but the battlefield was obscured with smoke, the men no longer responding to his instructions with the necessary speed. He watched as they fell, caught in crossfires or cut down by the mobile Liao horsemen. Worse, he had lost sight of Guiying. Worse than that even, the giant crossbow was not yet in position. There was heavy fighting around it and no sign of Lun.

'Your Excellency,' he said, 'we must think of your safety.'

The Emperor looked at him sternly. 'Do you think an Emperor less reckless than a girl?' he asked. 'You are my general. Lift your spirits. To win, you must do what is necessary.'

The General considered this. 'What would she do?' he murmured out loud. Making up his mind, he turned to the Emperor. 'Do you still have your sword, Excellency?'

The Emperor produced it from beneath his robe.

'Good. Then we abandon our post at once.'

In the end there were four of the Liao left standing. They faced her, panting and wary. Two held short double-edged swords, one a double-headed axe and one a spear.

In a group of four fighters there will always be one who is leader, two who instinctively work together, and one who hangs back, waiting. The axeman was the leader, she could tell at once. Without waiting for his attack, she tumbled forward, rose up in front of him too close for him to swing his weapon and knocked him out with a headbutt. The two swordsmen were already on her, working together, and she swivelled low to kick away the standing leg of the first, and, springing up, advanced on the second, rapidly boxing his ears. When his eyes began to roll back she punched him once with all her strength in the sternum between the nipples, and rapidly reverse-punched to crash her elbow into the chest of the second, just now leaping on her from behind. Sidestepping his falling body, she smashed her forearm into the side of his head, and he lay still on top of his companion.

Then there was only one left, the spearman. Facing him, she relaxed completely. She brought the palms of her hands together and began to bow respectfully. Confused, he instinctively began to do the same, and she caught him off-guard with a hook kick to the left side of the head. She blocked the thrust of his spear with a downward punch to numb his arm and, as he dropped his weapon, hit him with a back fist in the left eye. Staggering backwards, he fell on all fours in the dirt, looking at her helplessly.

She ran at him, and, as he shut his eyes in horror, she leaped onto his back and sprang off it onto a passing riderless horse.

A failure of the imagination is the worst fault on a battlefield. The Liao had not imagined her surviving the fight, let alone continuing her reckless advance. Unprepared, they allowed her to flash through their ranks – and in a matter of moments she faced Xiao Dalin on his black horse.

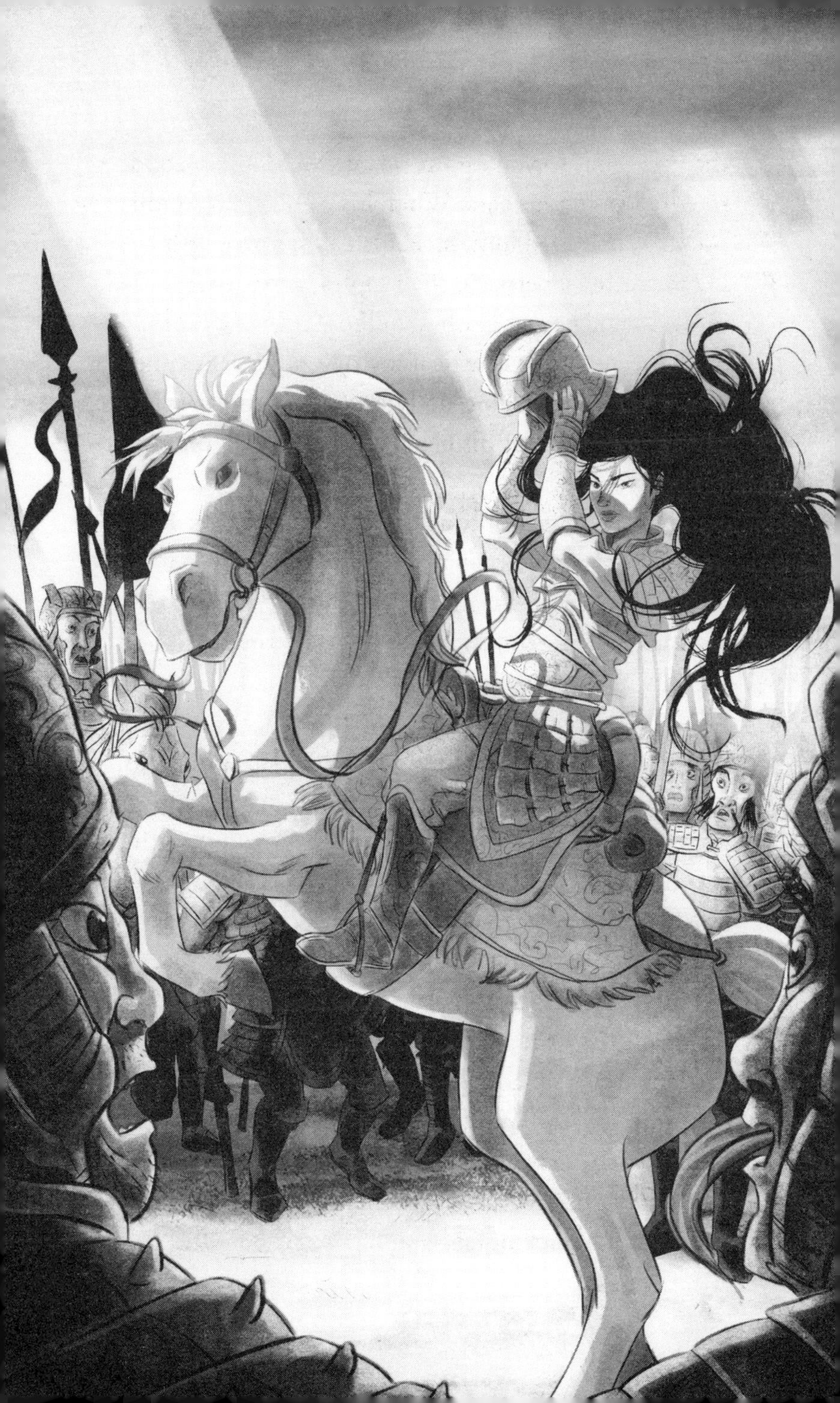

There was a moment of stillness as they looked at each other. Then she took off her helmet and shook her hair, and they all saw that she was a girl.

She called out to him, 'Your Empress Dowager has vowed to exterminate the Yangs. Well, the grandson of Yang the Invincible may be dead but the grandson's wife is *not*. I am a Yang too. But if you like,' she added, 'you can call me Mu Guiying, bandit's daughter.' She stood up in the stirrups, skimmed her helmet contemptuously at Dalin, and carelessly turned her horse away.

Behind her, she heard him come after her, and she kicked on her horse and flew back towards the Chinese lines, pursued by the furious Liao general and his commanders.

And now, she thought, all that matters is that Lun is ready.

Lun lay next to the giant crossbow. The Liao had gone, but so had his men, and the giant bow rested a few paces short of its necessary position. Dimly, through the foggy pain in his head, he heard the final drum signal but his legs didn't seem to be working properly.

He sat up, and fell over, and sat up again, slowly. Hauling himself upright, he leaned against one of the rear wheels of the cart and feebly pushed. There was a great pain in his shoulder and he moaned aloud.

But the pain invigorated him. He thought of his dead men, of the dead children of Nankou, and he gritted his teeth and heaved again.

The cart shifted a little and rocked backwards again.

Roaring, he pushed again. It went forward a half a pace and stopped.

Ahead of him there was a commotion, and he saw a figure on a horse speeding towards him pursued by fifty Liao horsemen, their general leading the way.

It was time.

But he had run out of time.

He heaved again, without effect. 'I have failed,' he said out loud.

'Nonsense,' said a brisk voice.

A fat man in a red robe spat on his hands and put his shoulder to the other rear wheel. At his other side the General bent to the axle.

There was no time for greetings.

'On a count of three,' the General said, calmly and orderly.

They heaved together and the cart finally moved forward, trundling heavily across the last few paces into position.

'Now what?' the Emperor asked.

'Now we fire,' the General said.

'At which of the enemy?'

He pointed. 'At her,' he said.

They all looked at Guiying bearing down on them at high speed.

'*What?*'

As the Emperor hesitated, Lun shoved him out of the way. 'Don't you trust her?' he shouted, and knocked away the firing pin, and they were all three thrown backwards as the enormous missile exploded from the bow with tremendous force and powered towards the girl on the horse not fifty paces away.

The double-prod bed crossbow fires bolts more than 2,000 paces at ten times the speed of a galloping horse. No one so near the bolt could possibly get out of its way after it was fired. Which is why Guiying had reached down to cut her saddle strap in the second before she saw Lun reach towards the firing pin. And by the time the bolt left the bow she had already begun to slide round the flank of the horse. And when, a microsecond later, the bolt shot over her horse, it only ripped off the right sleeve of her tunic and tore open her forearm.

But it utterly took out Xiao Dalin and a dozen of his commanders riding directly behind her, who never knew what had hit them.

Everything that day had led up to that moment. Nothing of the day was left afterwards. Without their general, the Heavenly Gate failed.

For a while Liao infantrymen stood confused and their cavalrymen rode in aimless circles, then they gathered their wits and fled the field. In the distance the red-lacquered sedan chair of the Empress Dowager was hastily carried away.

And alone and victorious on the deserted plain stood the men of China, and one girl.

25

GUIYING

It takes a moment to win a battle but months to negotiate the peace. Winter was over and spring had arrived by the time the treaty was signed in Bianjing. It was the month of the snake, in the eighth year of Emperor Zhenzong, and the plum blossom was out along the avenues of the Imperial capital when the ceremony took place before a crowd of thousands in the great courtyard outside the palace.

Under the terms of the treaty the Chinese would pay tribute to the Liao each year: 200,000 bolts of raw silk and 100,000 coins of silver. The Chinese took back their land.

Not everyone was happy with this. The Empress Dowager of the Liao, who was to die only four years later, opposed it. That stern old soldier General Yang didn't like it either. He thought the Liao, exhausted by war, could be finally defeated and their threat removed for ever. But his Emperor disagreed.

'The fruits of peace are worth more to us – and to the Liao – than any further fighting,' he said.

And for a generation both countries would grow rich on uninterrupted trade.

The General had to be content with a medal. Lun too. The Emperor presented them after the treaty was signed. It was a sad affair, though. The General could not forget the death of his only son, while Lun thought of his friends Ju and Ying and the children of Nankou Village who were avenged but who would never grow up.

'You both lived with your sorrow,' the Emperor said. 'And when your country needed you, you did not fail us. For this,' he said, hanging the medals around their necks, 'we are most truly grateful.'

They all stood a moment in silence, remembering.

'But I must ask,' the Emperor said, 'what has happened to the girl? I haven't seen her since she disappeared off the back of that horse.'

The General said, 'She is a Yang now. She has gone to guard your northern border.'

The Emperor nodded. 'Then my northern border is safe.'

And they went together into the palace for the feast.

* * *

But Guiying was not yet at the border.

She stood alone on a bare rock jutting from the cliffs above a green ravine where the fortress of Mu Ke lies hidden. The fortress was deserted now, slowly falling into ruin. Her father's men had all vanished, and there was nothing left of him but memories and the burial stone where he had departed the world with the help of the kindly vultures.

Standing there, as the sun set over the folded mountains, she gave thought to her husband, Zongbao, fallen to treachery at Yukou, and to the General, to Lun and the Emperor. She thought of her father, the fat old bandit. She was a Yang now but she remained who she had always been – light-hearted, firm, faithful to her own way of doing things. She had never needed praise, nor wanted medals, for they made nothing happen. She had given herself to the things that needed to be done.

She would pass lightly through life.

The sun had nearly set; shadows thickened the land. There were towns to rebuild, people who needed shelter, a border that still needed to be watched; and with a last look across the great downward sweep of forest, she turned to go.

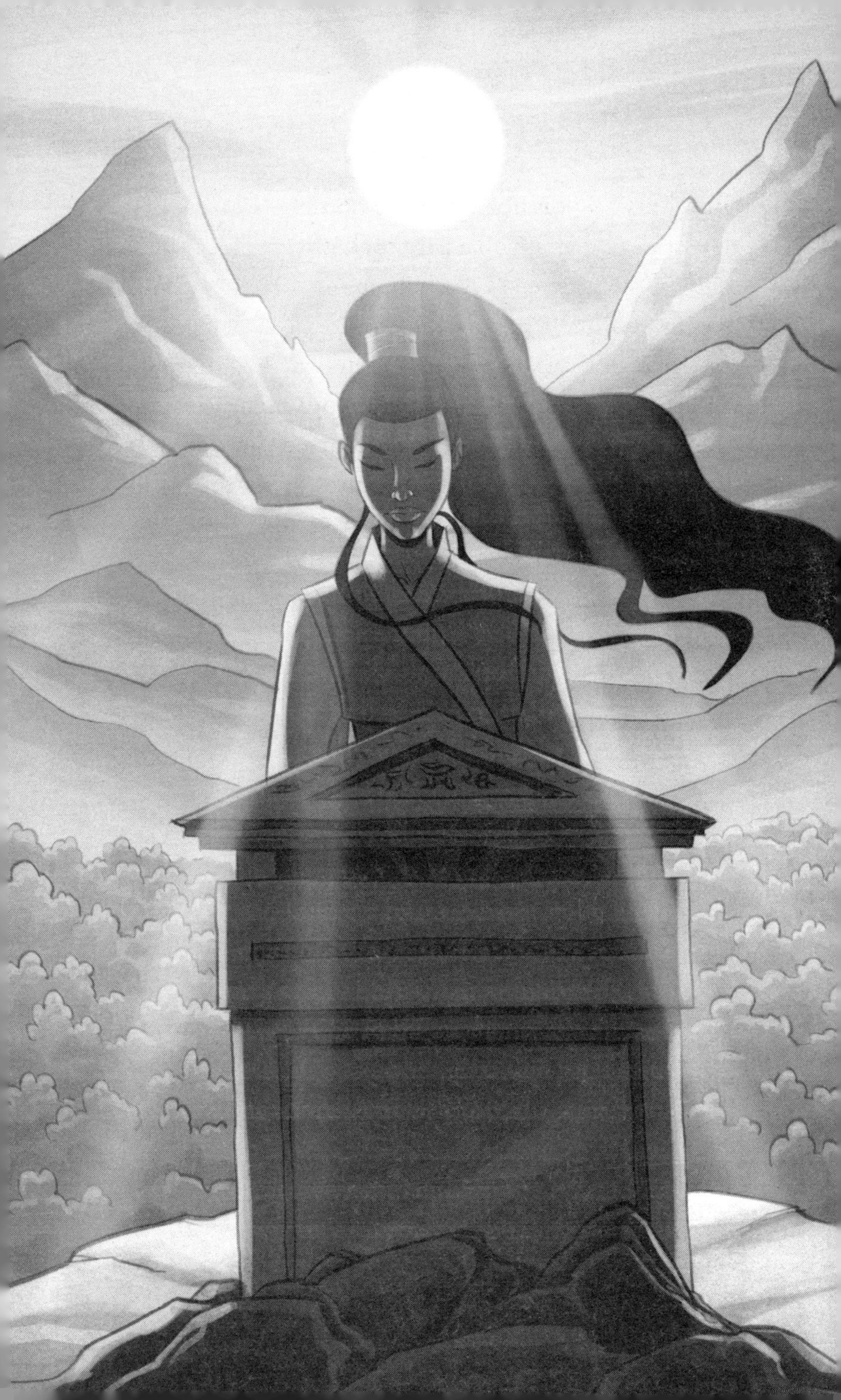

A LITTLE EXTRA ABOUT MU GUIYING AND CHINA

A LONG TIME AGO

China is one of the world's oldest civilizations. Gradually, over the years, villages and towns grew up there, beginning in the fertile plain of the Yellow River. For a long time these people didn't think of themselves as 'Chinese' – or indeed have any idea of a place called 'China'; they lived their lives in smaller communities and called themselves by different names. Local warlords fought each other for control over different regions.

By the year 1000, the time of our story, there were a number of well-established fighting factions, though none had control over all of modern China.

These included the people of the Song Dynasty, ruled by Emperors from the same family; their vast lands stretched from the eastern seaboard westward to the border with Tibet. To the north-west were the people of the Western Xia, a nomadic people also ruled by Emperors. And to the north-east were the Liao, nomads again, famous horsemen, great rivals of the Song. A prolonged war was fought between the Liao and the Song, with fighting heaviest along the mountainous border that separated them.

For a few generations this border was defended for the Song by a family of generals called Yang, whose extraordinary deeds were celebrated later in stories called *The Generals of the Yang Family*, an exciting mix of history and invention which captures the drama of the conflict.

MU GUIYING

She is one of the best-loved figures in China, the hero of numerous stories, operas, television shows and movies. There are temples dedicated to her. In the 1950s, the Communist leader Mao Zedong formed 'The Mu Guiying Brigade' for women to undertake great projects in the Chinese countryside. There is even a crater on the planet Venus named after her. But did she really exist?

All these events happened so long ago that it is hard to separate history from invention. There is certainly evidence for the existence of the Yangs and other characters and for the battles they fought. But it is clear now to modern historians that there is no hard evidence for Mu Guiying. Like King Arthur, it seems she is a legendary figure. She is the hero of folk tales based on history, tales which have been passed down and elaborated over hundreds of years, in which she has become – like Robin Hood – an inspiration for future generations.

TIMELINE

618–907 Tang Dynasty – powerful and prosperous, a golden age of poetry and painting

907–960 Era of The Five Dynasties and Ten Kingdoms – warlord fighting against warlord

916–1125 Liao Dynasty

960 Northern Song Dynasty established by Taizu, a brilliant general

976–997 Emperor Taizong – hard-working but unscrupulous; rumoured to have killed his older brother Taizu with an axe

997–1022 Emperor Zhenzong – made China richer but, like his father before him, struggled all his life against the horsemen from the north

980 Battle of Yanmen Pass – Yang Ye 'the Invincible' repels the Liao

986 Battle of Chenjiagu – defeated by the Liao, who were commanded by the Empress Dowager Xiao, Yang Ye is captured and starves himself to death

999 Battle of Suicheng – Yang Yanzhou 'the Peerless' defeats the Liao

1001 Battle of Yangshan – Yang Yanzhou again defeats the Liao

1004 Battle of Changyuan – the Liao general Xiao Dalin killed by a giant crossbow

1005 Treaty of Changyuan – peace between the Chinese and the Liao

1025 Peace ends when the Chinese join forces with the Manchu people to attack the Liao

HOW TO PRONOUNCE CHINESE NAMES AND PLACES

Changyuan	*Charng You En*
Chenjiagu	*Churn Jee-ah Goo*
Cao Bin	*Tsow Bin*
Daixian	*Die See-en*
Dongjing	*Dorng Jeeng*
Fu Xian	*Foo See-en*
Furong	*Foo Wrong*
Heng Shan	*Hurng Shan*
Jinyang	*Jin Yahng*
Liao	*Lee-ow*
Lu Zhong	*Loo Jong*
Mao Zedong	*Mow Tze Dong*
Mu Guiying	*Moo Gway Ing*
Mu Ke	*Moo Ker*
Mu Yu	*Moo Yoo*
Nankou	*Narn Koh*
Pan Mei	*Parn May*
Shanxi	*Sharn See*
Shizu	*Sher Tzoo*
Suicheng	*Sway Churng*
Wang Shen	*Warng Shern*
Wujiayao	*Woo Jee-ah Yow*
Xia	*See-ah*
Xiao Dalin	*See-ow Dah Lin*

Yandi	*Yen Dee*
Yang Yanzhou	*Yarng Jen Joe*
Yang Ye	*Yarng Yeah*
Yanmen	*Yen Murn*
Yukou	*Yoo Koh*
Zongbao	*Tzong Bow*

ACKNOWLEDGEMENTS

I'm deeply grateful to both Henrietta Harrison, Stanley Ho Professor of Chinese History at the University of Oxford, and Ms Niamh Calway, University of Oxford, for checking the factual content of my story. Slips and infelicities that may remain are, of course, entirely my own.

TRUE ADVENTURES

INCREDIBLE PEOPLE DOING INCREDIBLE THINGS

The most thrilling stories in history

QUEEN OF FREEDOM — Catherine Johnson — Defending Jamaica

THE GIRL WHO SAID NO TO THE NAZIS — Haydn Kaye — Sophie Scholl and the Plot Against Hitler

THE MYSTERIOUS LIFE OF DR BARRY — Lisa Williamson — A Surgeon Unlike Any Other

BANDIT'S DAUGHTER — Simon Mason — Kung Fu Girl in Ancient China

BLUE MOUNTAINS, WINDWARD JAMAICA, 1720

High above the army camps and plantations of the British Empire, a group of ex-slaves – called Maroons – are building a new home for themselves.

When British soldiers enter the forests to hunt them down, one of the Maroons will lead the fight against them – Queen Nanny, a 'wise woman' with a reputation for ancient obeah magic, and a guerrilla fighter of genius. Under her generalship, her people will make a do-or-die defence of their freedom.

NAZI GERMANY, 1942

As World War Two rages, Sophie Scholl reunites with her beloved brother Hans in Munich. Soon she meets his young student friends. Like her they can take no more of the war.

Then leaflets calling for a revolt against Hitler start appearing, put out by a mysterious group called the White Rose. Who are these people? No one knows. But the Gestapo is determined to hunt them down – and suddenly Sophie finds herself in the most terrible danger.

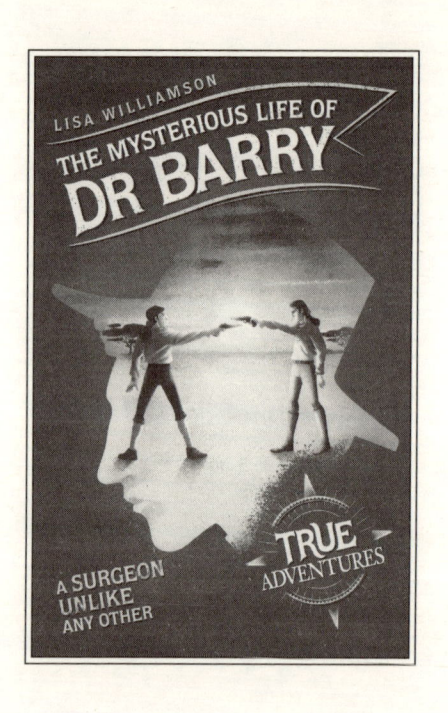

SOUTH AFRICA, 1808

Dr James Barry was Inspector General of Hospitals at the height of the British Empire, one of the most distinguished surgeons of his day, famous for his brilliance. In South Africa he carried out one of the world's first Caesarean operations in which both mother and child survived. He was also famous for his severity and prickly temper: when young he fought a duel and, in the Crimea, publicly delivered a rebuke to Florence Nightingale for lack of hygiene. Yet when his dead body was laid out an incredible secret was discovered about him.